Time Management for Families

The busy family's guide to finding balance and
calm in a hectic world

Bethany Fox

PARR PUBLISHING
L T D

Parr Publishing Ltd

Contents

Preface

When I announced to my friends that I had written my first book Mindfulness for Families, the immediate response from everyone was, "Where have you found the time?"

This question, asked in such incredulous voices and with such wonderment in their eyes, made me ask myself where on earth I actually had found the time. I have a full-time job, children at different stages in their education, each with several extracurricular activities to fit in, and a homestead with land, animals, and a vegetable garden to look after. On top of this, I volunteer for a local charity, I do at least an hour of exercise most days, I love to keep up with friends, and I take two or three trips abroad a year. Where did writing a book fit into my already busy schedule?

It's evident from my friends' reactions that everyone is busy. Everyone has hectic schedules, packed social calendars, and lots of responsibilities. Everyone wants to cram as much success and enjoyment into their lives as possible, which leaves little room for taking on that extra project that might give you renewed energy and joy for living. We are so busy staying in control and making everything perfect that we sometimes don't have time to connect with others or even our children. How often have you had a long-standing arrangement in the diary only for two or three guests to pull out last minute, citing they're tired or hadn't realized little Mason had a piano recital that clashed? We all have the same amount of time in our lives; it's what we do with it that makes a difference. We can't manage time as that's a constant; it's managing our lives that needs to improve.

In Time Management for Families, I'll share some of the tricks that work for me and examine some popular time management strategies. With a little planning and focus, these tips may help you reorganize your life, feel more in control, and have more freedom to connect with yourself, your friends, and your loved ones. And maybe you, too, will find the time to write that book you've always wanted to.

Chapter 1

Introduction

Managing family time can be a daunting task in today's fast-paced world. With the demands of work, school, extracurricular activities, extended family, and household responsibilities, there always needs to be more hours in the day. The pressure we place upon ourselves to succeed in all areas of life means we want to prove to ourselves that we can have it all and that our children can have it all too. We overcommit ourselves by agreeing to take on more than we can realistically handle. We juggle too many tasks at once so that when we accomplish a task, we're in such a rush that we only do it half-heartedly, creating more problems for ourselves further down the road. We overschedule, never leave enough time between appointments because we have so much to fit in, and rarely leave time to have fun with our children or connect with our partners. When something unexpected does arise, we can't handle it as our time is so stretched already. We micromanage, unable to delegate tasks, knowing that it is quicker and easier to do it ourselves. And we are perfectionists, forever worried about what others will think of us. Trying to do too much leaves us stressed, dissatisfied, and feeling out of control, and ultimately, we feel like failures. How can we fit everything in and come out on top?

With the rise of technology and social media, families now face new challenges that make it harder to disconnect and focus on what matters. We now have more distractions imposing on our limited time, making time management seem like even more of an elusive dream. An astounding 62.5% of people worldwide use the internet regularly; almost 5 billion people spend an average of seven hours online per day, and while over 90% of internet users have at least one social media profile, less than 18% use a dedicated time management system (Clockify, 2023). Despite having a wealth of knowledge at our fingertips, many of us still don't use it to find out how to use our time better. A 2022 study by Development Academy showed that 33% of people use a simple to-do list to manage their time, while 25% just do what "feels" important (Acuty Training, 2022).

There is a time management epidemic today caused by a lack of knowledge and the rise of technology which promotes a fast-paced "do-it-now" lifestyle. We were taught in school how to label a cell diagram and add and subtract but were never formally taught any time management skills. Despite having exams, extracurricular activities, family time, and social events to contend with, we had to figure it out on our own. It's no wonder many people today still rely on basic, ineffective techniques, like to-do lists and just dealing with things as they come. Time management feels like a fundamental construct that needs no research, study, or knowledge. However, if most of the world's topmost business leaders, political figures, and celebrities use time-management techniques to strategize their lives, then there must be something to it. After all, why would they bother learning this new skill if to-do lists worked just as well?

In this time-management epidemic, most families struggle to have enough time for even the most crucial things. We feed our children unhealthy meals because they are quick to prepare or easy to order. We miss a deadline because we are too busy ferrying our kids around. We're unlikely to grab an opportunity to learn a new skill or pursue a hobby because we're overcommitted elsewhere. Likewise, we often give up self-care in order to prioritize keeping the household running efficiently. We put off eating healthily, spending time together, spending time with friends, exercising, taking time out of our schedules, and looking after our mental health through a misplaced idea of having to act or appear a certain way.

These shortcuts to time management can be labeled "debtor's time," as we are only borrowing a debt on future time at a high-interest rate. For example, we may not have time to go to the gym regularly. While this saves a few hours a week, we may find that lack of exercise causes a health complication that requires us to visit a doctor for more hours a week than if we had just gone to the gym. Or we may neglect to spend time with our partner as we have so much else to do; this neglect may result in you drifting apart. Using debtor's time is like using a high-interest credit card to pay off a utility bill, and it will only cost you more.

The consequences of poor time management and using debtor's time can be significant. Families that don't prioritize time together may experience strained relationships, poor communication, and unhappiness (Ozbay et al., 2007). Children may feel neglected or isolated and start displaying behavioral problems (Miller et al., 2012) (Friedman, 2018). Likewise, parents may feel overwhelmed and stressed, leading to burnout and decreased productivity (Abramson, 2021). Ultimately, failing to manage family time effectively can harm the entire family unit (Flood and Genadek, 2016).

Children are at a pivotal stage in life where nearly every decision their parents make affects their future. The food they eat affects their development and how well they perform academically. The time they spend with their parents affects their emotional and social intelligence, which determines their future career and relationship outcomes. Children learn by observing and imitating the behavior of those around them, especially their parents, so it is critical to model the behavior we want them to emulate. As Pulitzer winner Carl Sandburg (Good Reads, 2023) said, "Time is the most valuable coin in your life. You and you alone will determine how that coin will be spent." As a parent, you also determine how to invest your children's coins to germinate the most interest and return for their future.

This book examines how to invest those coins for a more rewarding present and a brighter future. Rather than going into time debt, we will investigate how to heap the rewards of time management:

- Better quality family relationships.

- A stress-free, anxiety-free life.

- Better sleep.

- Improved focus.

- A healthier life.

With the freedom and knowledge you need to ditch your to-do lists, you can step into more sophisticated time management techniques that the experts use to reap magnificent gains. By learning the right tools and strategies, your family will be able to manage time more effectively and prioritize what truly matters. Plus, once you become "time-smart," your family can build stronger relationships, reduce stress, and achieve greater overall happiness and well-being. This book provides practical strategies for managing family time in the modern world, helping your family to thrive in today's do-it-now, 24/7 access society.

Chapter 2

Assessing

Do you ever have days where it seems you achieve very little, but time still speeds by? You may have a work deadline but keep getting distracted by calls, texts, and emails, so you end up working late and missing out on an evening with friends. Maybe you have a list of errands to run between dropping the children at various sporting activities, and you feel exhausted by the end of a day spent rushing about. Despite being busy, stressed, and with no time for ourselves, we often accomplish very little and still have a pile of responsibilities left to carry over to the next day. We can call it "trickle-down time." Although time seems to be trickling away slowly, it is still trickling through our fingers; leaving a tap dripping will still eventually flood your kitchen.

Time is like money, and even if you have a lot of it, a few purchases here and there add up. Likewise, with time, 20 minutes lost here and 10 minutes spent there add up, even though they seem like short amounts of time individually. When we work on trickle-down time, we accomplish very little each day, and our tasks continue to pile up until they eventually seem insurmountable. At this point, we either give up out of burnout or complete our tasks half-well in a misguided effort to get more done each day, which leads to more problems later on - problems that require more time to fix. To extricate ourselves from this cycle, we must first learn to assess our time usage.

Assessing your time usage allows you to gain a better understanding of how you are currently spending your time and identify areas where you can make improvements. By evaluating your time usage, you can determine if you are spending too much time on activities that are not productive or fulfilling and identify which activities are most important to you so you can prioritize them accordingly. You can identify areas where you can work more efficiently and create a more balanced schedule to ensure you are dedicating enough time to self-care, relaxation, and other beneficial activities. By taking the time to reflect on how you are currently spending your time and making adjustments where necessary, you can create a more balanced, enjoyable daily routine that supports your goals and values.

Assessing time usage is common sense. A thought as simple as: "Do I have enough onions to make this recipe?" is a form of determining our actions. We generally evaluate a product before we buy it; we may even shop around to get the best deal. We spend our money with care because it is a finite resource. The same should apply to time. The good news is that management skills we use in other parts of our life, for example, managing finances, can be easily transferred to time usage. We determine our household budget by tracking our monthly income and expenses, and the same skill applies to time.

Time Tracking

The best way to understand how your family spends time is to track your time. Time tracking is a management technique that involves noting everything you do in a day and how long it takes. It is similar to making a list of everything you buy and including the price of every item on the list.

Start by tracking your family's time usage for one week, or, if you want to understand better where your family spends the most and least amount of time, you could track your time for a month. As with anything that requires data, the more data you have, the better results you get. Use a time-tracking journal to help you with this activity.

Get everyone involved in time-tracking their day. Use printable worksheets to give to all family members to fill in and make it a fun game with prizes at the end of the week for the most fully completed sheet. The more detailed the notes, the more data we can collect and the better you can understand where you spend time. So, rather than writing "Took Jimmy to football: 2.5 hours," you could write something more specific like:

- Drove Jimmy to football: 15 minutes.

- Chatted to other parents and got coffee: 20 minutes.

- Watched the match: 1 hour.

- Had a post-match chat with parents while waiting for Jimmy to change: 10 minutes.

- Stopped for burgers on the way home: 30 minutes.

- Drove home: 15 minutes

Watching the match took only one hour, but the whole outing took more than twice that. Could you use the pre- and post-match time to do a more valuable activity like meal planning or listening to a podcast? Or you may feel that adult chatting time is good for your health. In that case, suggest a walk during the warm-up to exercise while catching up with the other parents. Is going for a post-match burger a regular activity or a one-off? If this is a regular activity, think about how you could better spend those two hours a month.

Another method to assess your time usage is to conduct a time audit, where you review your calendar, to-do list, and other records to determine how you are spending your time. Look for patterns and trends, such as which tasks take up the most time, when you are most productive, and when you tend to procrastinate.

To help you track your time, you can:

- Use apps such as Clockify and Toggl Track

- Use web applications, such as SlimTime.

- Keep a personal time log, such as using the notes app on your phone or journaling in a notebook. Use your notes to categorize your time, e.g., time spent driving to and attending extracurricular activities, time spent with extended family, time for leisure, time spent preparing for school, and so on.

Identify time wasters

Once the tracking process is complete, sit with your family members to assess how you spend your time. This process enables you to determine where you're using your time productively and how to replicate that in other aspects of life. It also helps you identify where you are wasting the most time so that you can come up with ideas on how to use this time more efficiently. It also offers you a chance to seek out times in your life that are beneficial but could be even more productive. In the example above, you identified a valuable time during your day (chatting with the other parents) that still has room for improvement (catching up while going for a walk).

Spend time with your family discussing this over a few days. Other family members might spot time wasters and opportunities for improvement in the family time map that you missed, and vice versa. Talk to your children about the importance of time management and the benefits of using their time effectively. Encourage them to reflect on how they are spending their time and to identify areas where they may be able to make improvements.

Bringing your kids in from the start of the process gives them a better understanding and background of what time management is and why it is crucial. By the time you get to the stage of implementing strategies for productivity, they will be more eager to be involved as they will feel ownership of some of the decisions.

Once you know how each family member uses their time, the next stage is to use specifically curated questions to challenge your thinking on how you use your time presently versus how you should use your time. The goal is to move out of the mindset of vague estimations and become more specific in your thinking and how you apply your time management.

Note that these are generalized questions that you can apply to your family's time use at the start of your time management journey. They set you in the right direction, empowering you to dig further into a time management lifestyle as it applies to your family's needs.

- What activities do you waste time on or spend a disproportionate amount of time on?

- Are there any activities and responsibilities where you could cut time?

- What activities do you spend the least amount of time on?

- What activities do you spend the least amount of time on that would benefit from extra time, for example, quality time spent with your partner?

- Do you get everything done by the end of the day?

- Which tasks require the most time? Is there a way to reduce some of the time you spend on these responsibilities without sacrificing productivity?

- Which responsibilities weigh on you the most psychologically and emotionally and cause you to procrastinate? Is there a way to use time management to reduce this toll? Is there a way to change your mindset so that these responsibilities no longer weigh on you?

- What activities and responsibilities can you combine? How can you multitask to save time?

- What periods are you and your family most susceptible to ego depletion? Ego depletion is the idea that we have a finite amount of willpower and self-control. Once we deplete this resource, we become more susceptible to being distracted, procrastinating, or simply not doing the tasks we should do.

- What time of day is each family member most productive? Can you include more responsibilities in that period without sacrificing productivity?

The beauty of time tracking is that it offers active, logical, data-driven facts and insights into how you spend your time.

Assessing and tracking your time are critical steps in effective time management. By evaluating how you're currently spending your time, you can identify areas for improvement, prioritize your tasks and responsibilities, and make more informed decisions about how to allocate your time and energy.

Reassess

Your family will go through regular changes that affect how successful your time management operations are. When you constantly reassess your techniques, their implementation, and your family's life stage, you ensure your goals are aligned. Essentially, after assessing your time management as a family, you need to regularly reassess, together with your family, how well your time management strategies are working. Regular reassessments are crucial to your family's success, even if your routines and needs don't change. It gives you a chance to take stock of what works and what doesn't from everyone's perspective.

Some of the questions you could ask are as follows: How happy do your children feel? Do they feel loved? Does your partner feel prioritized? Are you able to get enough sleep each night? Are your children doing well at school? Are you able to spend time with your family without stress? It is up to you and your family to determine what goals you want to meet, to discuss whether you are achieving these goals, and, if not, how to complete them better. If specific time management strategies work well, discuss with your family whether you should try to improve on them for better results or to leave them in place as they are.

Once you have assessed your time usage, you can begin to make adjustments to your routine to improve your time management skills. For example, you may eliminate time-wasting activities, delegate tasks, or set aside more time for self-care and relaxation. The key is to be intentional and mindful about how you spend your time and make adjustments as needed to ensure that you use your time in ways that support your goals and values.

Chapter 3

Goal Setting

To set goals for better time use, we need to think of time as a scarce resource, like money, energy, and power. We need to invest in scarce resources so they can work for us. If we invest in our time, we can make it work better for us.

According to research, "Valuing time with money is associated with greater happiness," (Whillans et al., 2016). People who value time above money enjoy improved well-being. Unsurprisingly, they also have healthier family relationships, higher job and academic satisfaction, and better social connections. These are all qualities that lead to more success in life for children and adults alike.

People who value time are more likely to prioritize responsibilities and tasks that are "intrinsically rewarding," leading to better mental and emotional health (Whillans et al., 2016). Just like money and other resources that we routinely use, time best serves us when we use it for responsibilities and activities that benefit us and to which we ascribe personal value and meaning. Going back to the example of walking while chatting to other parents at football practice, if you do not enjoy walking, then using your time for this activity is not prioritizing happiness. Instead, you could see if there is an outdoor fitness class nearby. Since your body and mind respond better to this sort of exercise, you have then found a way to prioritize not just your physical health but your mental and emotional health too. You can return to the game feeling good. Since you prioritized a task that is intrinsically rewarding to you, you now feel relaxed and calm and can better focus on your schedule, increasing your chances of meeting all your deadlines for the day. With this one change in your plan, you have significantly decreased your chances of carrying over responsibilities from one day to the next, moving out of debtor's prison and into time prosperity.

SMART goals

SMART goals are a fantastic option to empower you to dig further into your new lifestyle. SMART is an acronym that helps you nail down your goals. It stands for:

- Specific

Generalized, vague statements vary in how they apply to different people. If your time management goal is to, *"Spend more time with my kids,"* what does that mean exactly? To you, this could mean spending quality time with them every day, but to your partner, this could mean hanging out with them at the weekend. The same goal, applied to two people, means very different things, and you can avoid this by being very specific.

- Measurable

A goal is only a goal if you have a way to measure if you reach that goal. Estimations are often wrong, so measure things precisely. Using the goal of spending more time with your children, you could make your goal measurable by adding that you want to hang out with them every day, doing a fun activity for at least 10 minutes. A measurable goal allows you to easily track how much progress you are making toward your goal. Hence, if you cannot find 10 minutes a day, you can determine that you are not on target toward your goal and make changes to your plan or your execution.

- Attainable

You may love your kids and want to spend more time with them, but if your circumstances mean you only see them at weekends, a goal of spending time with them each day is unattainable. Ensure the goals you set are achievable.

- Relevant

Your goal has to serve a purpose in your life. Remember that time management is an investment. We invest because we want to bring even more value into our lives. You may decide that the opportunity to relax, unwind and have fun with your friends once a month is valuable to your family because it allows you to destress and take time off from thinking about your household responsibilities. By unwinding with your friends, you can come home happy, pleasant to be around, and more present with your family. In that case, your goal is relevant to your family, even if it takes you away from them once a month.

- Time-Bound

Lastly, your goals must have an end date, so you avoid procrastination. You can't simultaneously spread your time into many different investments. Reassess frequently if your time-management goals are successful and bring the value to your life that you designed them for.

Discuss your time use as a family and decide how to prioritize your regular tasks and responsibilities. The goals you believe to be relevant might only apply to some family members. This process of applying SMART goals to your time use should be carried out together as a family so that you can come to a consensus for everyone's benefit.

Time Blocking

Time blocking is a straightforward time management strategy that involves breaking your time into productive blocks. For example, you may need to clean the house at the weekend but still have a hectic schedule for that day. With time blocking, you give yourself precisely two hours (or however much time you need) to clean the house, leaving the rest of the day for the remainder of your tasks. It is an excellent strategy to use once you have determined all the time management goals with your family.

When you time block, you cannot do anything else during that block. If you have given yourself 30 minutes to do yoga, you cannot check your phone, make a cup of tea, or do anything else non-essential during those 30 minutes. The idea is that by focusing every bit of time, energy, and attention on that activity, you are less distracted, less likely to procrastinate, and, as a result, more likely to complete the task within that period. Time blocking also prevents you from multitasking when carrying out urgent tasks that need all your focus.

You can time block your entire day's schedule, or you can choose to time block only particular tasks to complete that day. It is up to you to decide which method works better for you. I time block the first two hours of the day from 6am. I know I have two hours to get my workout done, to hang out the laundry and to shower and get dressed for the day. Knowing I need to achieve this by 8am makes me focus on the tasks in hand and not get distracted by the demands of kids or the pull of my phone. The kids can wait until 8am when I can give them my undivided attention, as I know the next hour is for them alone.

Here is an example of a time-blocked morning schedule:

- *6:00 am - 7:00 am Get up and go for a run.*

- *7:00 am - 7:45 am Shower and get dressed.*

- *7:45 am - 8:40 am Take children to school.*

- *8:40 am - 9:00 am Drive to work.*

- *9:00 am - 9:30 am Check and respond to emails.*

- *9:30 am - 10:30 am. Meeting with a client.*

- *10:30 am - 12:00 am Complete project by the deadline today.*

To help you with time blocking, you can use good time-blocking apps, such as Sunsama, Tick Tick, and Sorted Ap.

When time blocking, ensure you don't fill all the space in your schedule. Allow for some gaps at strategic points during the day because no matter how well you plan, unexpected events can occur. Maybe you'll get a phone call from school asking you to come and pick up your child. Or maybe a colleague requires some urgent help meaning you have to delay your own work. Leaving some open space in your schedule allows you to plan for these eventualities without throwing off your entire day. Leaving space in your schedule also allows you to take breaks to recharge and refocus without falling behind on your work. Sometimes, the best ideas come when you're not actively working on something and an open space in your schedule will give you time to think creatively and come up with new ideas. Trying to cram too much into your schedule can lead to burnout and fatigue so scheduling some open space means you can avoid overworking yourself and ensure that you have time for self-care and relaxation.

The Eisenhower Matrix

Another time management method, the Eisenhower matrix, is one of the most popular time management strategies because it is so effective (Scroggsa, 2023). It allows you to prioritize your tasks according to how important and urgent they are. By classifying each task into one of the four categories, you can decide which ones to complete first and which to finish last.

In a 1961 address to the Century Association, former US president Dwight D. Eisenhower, inventor of the Eisenhower method, said: "Who can define for us with accuracy the difference between the long and short term! Especially whenever our affairs seem to be in crisis, we are almost compelled to give our first attention to the urgent present rather than to the important future" (Scruggs, 2014).

Eisenhower's matrix revolutionized time management because it teaches us that the tasks we think of as important are often not urgent, while the tasks we think of as urgent are often not important. Problems arise because humans tend to complete tasks that we deem urgent first (Griffeth, 2023). However, since we often wrongly categorize non-urgent tasks as important, we find ourselves completing non-urgent tasks first, based on this erroneous categorization.

What is so revolutionary about the Eisenhower matrix is that it is so effective yet so simple. It only requires that you draw a table like the one below:

	Urgent	Not urgent
Important	Do the tasks classified as urgent and important now.	For tasks that are not urgent but still important, schedule a time for them, preferably using time blocking. Complete these tasks only after you have finished the urgent and important tasks.
Not Important	You can delegate urgent but not important tasks to someone else. These tasks can often be given to your children as chores or completed by you when you are less busy during the day.	These tasks are a waste of time because they are neither urgent nor necessary. Your social media app messenger notifying you that someone commented on a picture of yours is not urgent or important. While you may want to respond to that comment, choosing to do so is only pulling away your time, energy, and effort from urgent and important tasks. You will find that these types of functions also end up distracting you and wasting your time during the day. Logging into social media to do just one thing is a lie we all tell ourselves because there will always be another post that grabs our attention.

Once you use the SMART method to record your goals, you can then use these goals to determine the types of jobs you need to complete weekly. In essence, your long-term responsibilities are your SMART goals, while your short-term responsibilities should be on your weekly to-do list. Incorporate your weekly to-do list into the Eisenhower matrix listing the tasks you need to accomplish. SMART goals determine how you categorize each task on the Eisenhower matrix. For example, if you are a parent of a newborn, two of your SMART goals could read as follows:

1. Take care of my newborn, meeting all emotional, physical, mental, and developmental needs.

2. Continue to spend time with my partner so that we do not drift apart, and we can continue to be sources of emotional and social support for each other as new parents.

In this case, your Eisenhower matrix for the day may then read something like this:

	Urgent	Not urgent
Important	• Feed my baby as many times as needed.	• Do the laundry, wash all the soiled clothes, and dry them for use throughout the week. • Partake in tummy time with my baby. • Bath my baby. • Respond to work emails. • Respond to my health insurance company. • Chat with my partner about how they're handling parenting. Offer emotional support by listening and encouraging.
Not important	• Mop the floors in the kitchen and bathroom. • Video call grandma so she can see her great-grandchild for the first time.	• Buy new kitchen towels to replace the old ones. • Buy some green tea. • Watch that comedy video my fitness instructor sent me about gym etiquette.

The Eisenhower matrix is a great tool to avoid ego depletion because it forces you to carry out essential and urgent tasks before you reach the point where your ego begins to deplete. It also allows you to delegate some tasks to others, so you carry only a few responsibilities. Lastly, it enables you to recognize tasks that are neither urgent nor important so that you can reserve your time and energy for more pressing obligations.

***

By setting goals for your family, you can ensure that everyone is on the same page, working towards a common vision, and making the most of their time together. Since time is finite, we can use SMART goals to set our intention for our time and to prioritize what responsibilities and tasks we spend our time on. Time blocking is a straightforward time management strategy involving breaking your time into productive blocks. The Eisenhower matrix is a popular time management tool because it is so effective at allowing you to prioritize your tasks according to how vital they are. Goal setting is an essential aspect of family time management, providing direction and focus, encouraging collaboration and communication, prioritizing family time, providing a sense of accomplishment, and fostering growth and development. By setting goals for your family and working towards them together, you can make the most of your time together and build a stronger, more connected family.

Chapter 4

Teamwork

Before civilization began and we thought up the ideas of society, life was tough. Without opticians, the short-sighted man was forced to squint day and night and hope that a predator wouldn't sneak up on him. Without blacksmiths, it was up to each person to sharpen their knives if they were going to catch any dinner. Each person had to do it all if they were to survive. As social animals, we need to pull together and use each person's strengths for the good of the community. We need each other to survive. We need everyone in our community to pull their weight and add their contribution; otherwise, we all fail. The same principle applies to families.

Family communities need the support of every member because they cannot do it alone. Just like time, human energy and effort are finite and will eventually run out so we have to rely on teamwork. When we divide our tasks and responsibilities, we conquer them with ease.

Divide and Conquer

Before you divide tasks up within the family, have a conversation with your partner and any other adult family member living with you about how to divide up the urgent and essential tasks and responsibilities amongst yourselves. Earlier, you made a list of everyone's weekly activities. Inputting the list into the Eisenhower matrix is a constructive way to visualize what tasks you may need to eliminate (the not-important and not-urgent ones). That way, you reduce items on your to-do list, giving everyone in the family breathing space

Once all your tasks are on the Eisenhower matrix, you can share out the tasks bearing your SMART goals and your strengths and weaknesses in mind. For example, if your partner enjoys being outdoors, they could take on responsibility for mowing and window cleaning.

How to encourage children to participate

One of the most challenging aspects of managing family time is balancing household chores with other responsibilities. Involving kids in household chores can lighten the load and teach your children valuable life skills. If you have included your children in the time management process from the start, they will be more eager to take on their part of the family's responsibilities. Children pull their weight if they understand that everyone is doing their part to keep the household running smoothly, and when this becomes a habit, it is very time efficient. However, some kids need more encouragement than others to do their chores.

Here are some strategies to encourage your kids to help with household duties consistently:

- Set up a written contract with your child with your expectations. Craft this contract together with your child, including things like what tasks they need to carry out every day (e.g., make bed, get bag ready for school, set the table, empty the dishwasher, feed/walk the dog) and what tasks they must carry out weekly (e.g., water plants, mow lawn, sort laundry, etc.).

- Emphasize that part of growing up living in your household means that they need to contribute to the family's well-being, and they can pitch in by doing their part, just as you do your part.

- Ensure that your child knows what contributions the adults make and how much time this takes each week (e.g., cooking, cleaning, folding clothes, driving to sporting fixtures, etc.). A good way to emphasize this is to involve them in these activities so they realize how much energy, effort, and time it takes you to accomplish.

- Ensure you reward your child with gratitude for their contribution to the household. Make a point of regularly saying, "Thank you, your help makes such a difference to me." This positive reinforcement is very motivating.

- Don't offer money in exchange for completing tasks around the house. If you add a monetary value to these contributions, your child will ONLY help if they're getting paid. You also teach them they must expect a financial reward for being responsible. If you decide to give your children money, give them a no-strings-attached allowance instead.

- Make it fun and engaging. Household tasks don't have to be a chore. Make cleaning fun by turning it into a game or competition. For example, set a timer and challenge your kids to see who can clean their room the fastest. Use upbeat music to create a lively atmosphere while cleaning.

- It's never too early to start teaching kids about responsibility and the importance of contributing to the household. Even toddlers can help with simple tasks like putting away toys or clothes, and as children get older, you can gradually increase their responsibilities.

- Be Clear and Specific. To avoid confusion and frustration, clearly communicate the expectations for each chore. Give specific instructions and demonstrate how to complete the task. Training your child on how to complete each task proficiently will save you time in the long run.

- Assigning household chores fairly can avoid sibling rivalry and prevent burnout. Divide duties based on age, ability, and interest. For example, a younger child may be responsible for setting the table, while an older child may be responsible for cleaning the bathroom. Depending on what works for you, either rotate chores regularly to keep things fair or give your children sole ownership of their tasks.

- Lead by Example. Children learn by watching their parents, so be a good role model by doing your share of the household chores. Show enthusiasm for cleaning and involve your kids in your cleaning routines. Appreciate your kids' contributions and thank them for their hard work.

Sharing tasks with your children frees up your time for the important and urgent tasks in your household and gives you a sense of freedom that the chores are not all your responsibility. Giving children age-appropriate chores teaches them responsibility and accountability, which helps to build their self-esteem and confidence. They learn essential life skills such as cleaning, organizing, and cooking which will help them become more self-sufficient as they grow older. Involving children in household chores teaches them the value of working together as a team which can improve their communication skills and foster a sense of community within the family. They also learn the value of hard work and the satisfaction of a job well done which can instill a strong work ethic that will serve them well throughout their lives. By having a set of chores to complete, children learn how to manage their time effectively which will be a valuable skill for them as they grow older and must balance school, work, and other responsibilities.

Overall, involving children in household chores benefits their personal growth and development. It teaches them essential life skills, helps build their self-esteem and work ethic, and fosters a sense of teamwork and responsibility within the family.

Building a Support Network

Family is a community where every member chips in to keep the unit thriving. However, we often need a broader community around us to survive. Many of us today have nuclear families composed of two adults and (typically) 1-4 kids. The nuclear family is a startling change from families of the past, where grandparents, uncles, aunts and cousins lived together and shared life as a family unit.

The joy of living with an extended family is that time management becomes much more accessible as there is always someone with whom we can share responsibilities. With the rise of the nuclear family, it is now up to us to develop an extended family by building a support network around us. A support network gives many options for outsourcing and delegating help. For instance, we could ask for help from friends and families or share school responsibilities with other parents to lighten the load of being a parent and build stronger relationships. A support network can help during emergencies or when we cannot effectively meet all our tasks.

Research has shown that people with strong, supportive social networks live healthier and longer lives. With a support network, we feel less stress because people are always there to lend a helping hand when life gets too much. Recent research states, "The survival of humans depends on their effective social functioning. Caregiving and attachment are key elements of parental love that are essential not only for survival during infancy and childhood but also for physical and psychological well-being throughout life,"(Vila, 2021).

Building a community of allies comes easily to some. Typically, people who grew up with an extensive support network are better able to construct a strong support group around them because they picked up these skills from childhood. For others, it can be daunting. Learning how to trust other people, showing vulnerability, and delegating are all complex tasks when you want to remain in control. We want to be able to do it all and fear being unable to cope on our own. However, it is worth trying to overcome these fears because, as well as giving practical assistance, your network can help reduce stress and provide emotional support and encouragement.

Your social support network only needs to include a few people you trust to be there for you when you need help: people who will uplift you in your time of need. It could include two close friends or just one or two family members. However, it is beneficial to have more people in the group so there are different people in your support network with diverse skill sets and qualities who can meet your various needs. You may have a relation who is excellent at offering comfort when you need it and always seems to have time for you. You may have a friend who has a childcare background and is very good at looking after your children when you're unable to get home on time.

To build your support network, you may have to meet new people or get closer to people you already know. It's a process that requires a fair bit of vulnerability but is ultimately very rewarding. Most people can find friends and support from places like work, church, hobby groups, exercise groups, volunteering, book clubs, and so on.

Choose people for your support network who fit in with your values and are on your wavelength, as they will be a part of your life and your children's lives. They need to be emotionally and socially capable and treat people with compassion, kindness, and respect. Do they stand up for you and listen to you without judgment when you need to talk through problems? The more emotionally and socially intelligent a person is, the more skilled they will be at providing you with social and emotional support when needed.

Your support network can help you lighten the load of life's responsibilities in the following ways:

- Picking up your kids from school and extracurricular activities.

- Cooking, shopping, and other housework for you and your family when you are sick or too busy with a significant life event.

- Babysitting.

- Listening when you need someone to talk to or comfort you.

- Giving your children other adult time - grandparents are great for this.

- Offering financial support when money is tight.

- Offering advice when you are going through something they have life experience in.

When building a support network, accept that this means you also need to assist the other person from time to time. There will be times when your Eisenhower matrix will have tasks on the top row for the benefit of your support network rather than for you. To be a good support network for others, you need to spend some time building these relationships.

In summary, involving your children in household chores will reduce the number of responsibilities you have and teach your children valuable life skills; and building your own support network can be crucial in helping to run your life. In short, teamwork is an essential aspect of family life, as it allows family members to work together towards common goals, support each other, and make the most of their time together.

Chapter 5

Technology

Technology has revolutionized many aspects of our daily lives, and family life is no exception. From parenting and education to communication and leisure, technology has transformed the way we approach and experience our lives. Today, we have access to an array of technological tools and resources that help us save time, stay connected, and enhance our overall quality of life.

With the advent of smartphones, tablets, and other mobile devices, families are more connected than ever before. Parents can track their children's development and health through mobile apps, stay in touch with relatives across the globe via video calls, and manage household tasks through smart home devices. Technology has also changed the way we learn and teach, with online learning platforms and educational apps providing new opportunities for children to engage with educational materials and explore their interests. At the same time, technology has also presented new challenges and considerations for families. The potential negative effects of technology on family life, such as screen addiction and social isolation, have sparked important conversations and debates about the role of technology in family relationships. As such, it's important for families to approach technology use mindfully and intentionally, setting boundaries and maintaining balance to ensure that technology enhances, rather than detracts from, their family life.

Automation

Automation refers to the use of technology and software to automate tasks and processes that would otherwise be performed manually by humans. The goal of automation is to increase efficiency, reduce costs, and improve accuracy by eliminating the need for human intervention in repetitive or time-consuming tasks. Automation can help us save time when managing our work and home lives, and it can also reduce human error.

Technology can automate many tasks that previously required significant time and effort. For example, using a meal planning app can save time spent on grocery shopping and meal preparation, while using a smart home device can automate household tasks like adjusting the thermostat and turning off lights. Technology can also help families manage household tasks more efficiently, from online shopping and grocery delivery services to smart home devices that automate tasks like cleaning and organization. Here are some of the apps, websites, and gadgets that can make family life easier to manage.

- An intelligent home system, such as the Vivint Smart Home, helps you control your heating system remotely. It also comes with a doorbell camera with a 180° x 180° doorbell field of view, smart lock, and security sensor so you keep your children safe if you leave them alone for a few hours. Plenty of intelligent home systems are available to you, so make sure you shop around to find one that suits your family's needs.

- Roomba or other robot vacuum cleaners. These can be pro-grammed to clean at night so you wake up to crumb-free floors, and they are arguably better cleaners than humans as they easily fit under beds and sofas. There are similar robots that mop floors and even clean windows. You can also purchase two-in-one brooms and mops, such as the iRobot Braava Jet m6.

- Multipurpose tabletop ovens, such as The Anova Precision oven, allow you to roast, bake, steam, or slow cook in one handy table-top oven. Your older children can use these cookers to warm up frozen food or to cook quick meals and snacks. To make it safer for your kids, you can purchase an app-controlled one that you can control even when you are away. Multipurpose cookers also save you time because you are only cleaning one device, despite using it for many purposes.

- Intelligent displays, such as Amazon Echo or Google Nest Hub, are handy for kitchen tasks and responsibilities. You can leave them on your kitchen countertop and then quickly find recipes, conversion charts, timers, music, etc., without touching them. You can use these voice-controlled devices to curate your shop-ping list. If you open your fridge and realize you have run out of milk, you can voice command your display to add it to your list for the next time you go grocery shopping.

- Home fitness gadgets, such as an exercise bike or treadmill can be incorporated into a home gym. A home gym can cut out time traveling to the gym and you can be at home to watch your chil-dren while keeping your health in great shape. A home gym might seem like an expensive investment, but the amount you spend initially covers a year or two of gym memberships, meaning that you save plenty of money over the long term.

- Time-saving kitchen devices are often a healthy and cheaper way of cooking and can be safe for children to use. Gadgets include:

  - Boiling hot water tap, e.g., a Quooker

  - Airfryer

  - Instant pot

  - Slow cooker

  - Microwave

  - Steamer

  - Soup maker

- Online doctor appointments will save you the time of driving there. Wearable health-tracking devices keep on top of your health and alert you of health issues that you can fix before they become big time-wasting problems.

- Many online grocery subscription plans will send you monthly groceries that your family uses regularly.

- Family organizer apps, such as Cozi, TeuxDeux, and Toodledocan help you manage your time.

- Regular traffic updates on your phone to help you avoid traffic, from apps such as Wazcan save you time in traffic and help you plan your route.

- Meal prepping apps, such as Big Oven, Lala Breakfast, and Pinterescan give you inspiration when meal planning.

- Grocery list apps like Remember The Milk help you remember what groceries you need.

- Chore apps, such as ChoreMonster, BusyKid, and OurHome, assign chores to your kids to help them organize and complete their household responsibilities.

- Apps like TeamSnap help you organize your kids' team sports with other team parents.

- Get help in planning your calendar precisely, with apps such as Hub Family Calendar Organizer and Flayk.

- Hire a Virtual Assistant to help you organize emails, make calls, schedule appointments, arrange travel and order groceries on websites such as Zirtual and Upwork.

How to Embrace Technology

If the above list of apps and gadgets fills you with dread and makes you think, "I'm no good with technology, I'll leave that part out," then stop, take a breath, and try to have an open mindset. Virtually everyone has a mobile phone these days, and we can use this all-encompassing gadget to start small.

I love my phone for its ability to streamline and communicate. Having a shared calendar with the rest of the family keeps me up-to-date and in control of all the activities going on. I have access to a wealth of information that I can dip into when I have five minutes to spare. I listen to training videos or podcasts when I'm out for a run and I can keep up to date with the news, the weather, the exchange rate, what's in stock at the library, what energy our solar panels are generating, and a whole host of other information just by clicking into a different app.

Similarly, I love my household gadgets which save me time, effort, and money in the long run. I set my robot cleaner to clean the floors at night, I throw some ingredients into the slow cooker in the morning to save prep time for tonight's dinner, I use my soup maker at lunch for a steaming bowl of soup with no fuss and I have a home gym which means I save the time it would take traveling to the gym in town and also means I can exercise first thing in the morning when my kids are in bed.

Start by experimenting with a few basic apps or tools, and gradually add more as you become more comfortable. If you're feeling overwhelmed or unsure about how to use technology for time management, don't be afraid to seek help and guidance. This may involve consulting with tech-savvy friends or family members, taking online tutorials or courses, or working with a professional coach or mentor. Basics such as learning how to delete apps, unsubscribe from emails, and turn off notifications, can have an enormous impact on our efficiency and well-being. Rather than focusing on the potential risks or drawbacks of technology, try to focus on the benefits. Think about how technology can help you be more productive, organized, and efficient, and how it can help you achieve your goals. Here are some ways you can use your smartphone to manage your time:

- Smartphones come with built-in calendar apps that allow us to schedule and manage our appointments, meetings, and other important events. By using these apps, we can avoid scheduling conflicts and make sure we have enough time to complete our tasks. We can have separate calendars for work, our social lives, and our kids' activities or you can put all the activities into one calendar and share it with the whole family so everyone knows what's going on each day.

- By using built-in to-do list apps that allow us to create and manage our daily tasks, we can break down our larger goals into smaller, more manageable tasks, and prioritize them based on their importance and urgency.

- Smartphones also come with built-in note-taking apps and reminder features that allow us to capture and store important information and ideas. By using these tools, we can quickly jot down ideas or important details and set reminders to follow up on them later.

- Many smartphones also come with cloud storage options that allow us to store and access our files, photos, and other important information from anywhere, when we have an internet connection.

- The Voice Control function lets us dictate commands, send messages, open apps and make calls hands-free which can be a great time saver when you are on the move, cooking, or busy with other tasks.

Smartphones are incredibly powerful tools that can help us save time in many different ways. By taking advantage of the features and apps available to us, we can streamline our daily tasks, stay organized, and be more productive in both our personal and professional lives.

However, we must be mindful of the potential pitfalls of using technology and make it work for our own situation. If you are stressed out by the constant bleeping, flashing, and demands made on you by WhatsApp groups, turn the notifications off. If you get sucked into mindlessly scrolling through social media on your breaks, delete the apps or give yourself a strict limit of 15 minutes a day as a wind down in the evening. With so many apps, notifications, and alerts competing for our attention, it can be difficult to stay focused and avoid distractions. Try to avoid the increased stress, fatigue, and even burnout that digital overload can bring by having days off technology where you just go out with your family and have a day in the fresh air. Technology can certainly help us stay connected and collaborate in real time, but it's important to remember the value of human connection and face-to-face communication. Overreliance on technology may lead to a lack of personal connection and may even hinder our ability to build strong relationships with others.

Technology can be challenging, but it's important to approach it with an open mind and a willingness to learn. Try to stay curious and open to new ideas and approaches and be willing to experiment and try new things. It's important to take a mindful approach to technology use so try to be intentional and deliberate about how you use technology, setting boundaries and limits as needed, and regularly evaluating its effectiveness. By approaching technology use mindfully, you can avoid the potential risks and drawbacks while maximizing its benefits.

Chapter 6

Advanced Planning

The more you plan, the better prepared you are for the future. As Benjamin Franklin said: "By failing to prepare, you are preparing to fail." This chapter explores how to use advanced planning as a tool to improve time management skills further and to help you carve out extra time in your schedule for important events and additional responsibilities.

We already saw that trickle-down time involves wasting 10 minutes here and 20 minutes there, only to suddenly realize it has all added up by the end of the day. Likewise, when you save 10 minutes here and 5 minutes there, not only are we saving time, but we are also avoiding debtors' time, meaning that we are not borrowing on future time at high interest.

When you start being more productive with your time whether it be multitasking through your small pockets of spare time (think of completing a brain training activity while at the bus stop), assessing your time, goal setting, or actively not wasting time (think of bored scrolling through social media) you will be benefit in the following ways:

- Less stress deciding what tasks and responsibilities to prioritize.

- Motivation to track your time management progress.

- More mental space leading to fewer mistakes in your day-to-day activities.

- Better routine, teaching you to be disciplined and structured with your time.

- Fewer conflicts and rushing that comes from being disorganized.

- Building your knowledge on how long your usual tasks take creating more time for spontaneity and fun.

- Building your reputation as reliable and proficient while also making you successful in your tasks which, in turn, opens up more opportunities for you.

- Structuring your goals and making them well-defined making you more likely to accomplish them.

- Preventing panic when the unexpected happens. If failing to prepare causes you to fail, then preparing causes you to succeed even when plans along the way fail.

Let's explore some advanced planning techniques, so you can begin to collect interest on your time savings.

Meal Prepping

Meal prepping is a widespread practice of preparing meals in advance to make mealtime more convenient and efficient. It involves planning, shopping, and cooking meals for a week or more in advance, then portioning and storing them in containers for easy access and consumption.

Meal prepping is the new "it" time management hack nowadays. You can't browse social media for more than a minute without seeing some delicious food being prepared and divided evenly into separate food containers. It is popular due to its numerous benefits, including saving time and money, promoting healthier eating habits, reducing food waste, and reducing stress.

One of the most significant benefits of meal prepping is that it saves time as you only need to cook once or twice a week. Meal prep can be beneficial for busy parents who may lack time or energy to cook after a long day at work or when there are after-school activities to navigate. By planning meals, you can make a shopping list and buy what you need, reducing the likelihood of impulse purchases. Buying in bulk can save you money in the long run, and you can also take advantage of sales and discounts. Additionally, by taking your food to work or school, you can save money on buying expensive lunches.

Meal prepping can also promote healthier eating habits and reduce food waste. By planning your meals, you can ensure you get all the nutrients you need and avoid unhealthy options. Preparing your meals allows you to control the portion size and the quality of ingredients to avoid the excess salt, sugar, and unhealthy fats found in many processed foods. By planning meals, you can use up ingredients before they expire, and you can also use leftovers to create new meals rather than throwing away food, which can be both wasteful and expensive.

Finally, meal prep can reduce stress. By having meals ready and waiting, you can avoid the last-minute rush to put together a meal, which can be particularly stressful when you're tired or busy. Knowing that you have healthy, delicious meals waiting for you can help you feel more in control and less stressed overall. Meal prepping also removes that stage of meal planning where you have to decide what meal to cook tonight, what ingredients you have and need to purchase on your way home, what your family would like to eat tonight, and so on. Going through this cycle every day drains mental energy, time, and money. The more often you prepare meals in advance, the more options you have for your family to choose from, removing the need to prepare new meals every day.

To meal prep, take some time when you are less busy to plan your meals and grocery list for the week ahead. The brilliance of meal prepping is that you can arrange two or more meals with some of the same recipes to save time picking out items at the grocery store and preparing ingredients. For example, if one of your main ingredients for dinner includes carrots and tomatoes, you can decide on a breakfast meal that includes tomatoes and a lunch meal that includes carrots. This method also slashes your food preparation time and the time it takes to clear out the fridge of unwanted or spoiled food regularly.

Spending two hours at the weekend prepping meals for the week saves you from spending 30 minutes each night making dinner for your family. That means, each week, you save 1.5 hours which amounts to 78 hours annually. With 78 extra hours a year, you could:

- Sleep an extra 15 minutes daily, giving yourself the rest you need to be resourceful and finely tuned at home and work.

- Take a weekend break with your family to unwind and relax.

- Download and sign up for the apps and websites you need to manage time effectively.

- Go shopping for all your meal-prepping essentials with enough time to go on your annual school essentials shopping trip with your kids.

- Declutter your home, making cleaning easier and faster for the rest of the year.

- Spend some time unwinding by reading a good book or watching a series.

- Prepare for and go on several date nights with your partner.

- Plan your family's annual financial budget and monthly schedules.

- Volunteer your time to give something back.

- Become competent in a new hobby or skill.

When you first begin meal prepping, you must ensure that you prepare enough meals to have a variety for a few weeks. As the weeks go by, you will naturally acquire more options because of the meals prepared in previous weeks.

Choose recipes with ready-to-cook ingredients, for instance, frozen vegetables, store-bought stock, pre-chopped onions, etc. Prepare smoothie packs for breakfast or lentil soup for dinner, and pop them into the freezer until you are ready to use them. Not all food needs to go in the freezer. You could prepare something like carrot slices with hummus for lunch, which could go in the fridge for a few days.

An alternative to meal prepping is to prepare ingredients in advance, for example chopping up all your vegetables and then storing them in the fridge or freezer, which cuts down on your actual food cooking time. Preparing ingredients is very useful if you grow your own fruit and vegetables.

Groceries

Forgetting to buy one item during the weekly grocery shopping can be a big time waster if you then have to make a specific trip back to the store. To avoid wasting time on repeat supermarket runs, consider the following:

- Make a list of all the staple items your family needs and place them on a subscription online grocery delivery list or keep a copy in your wallet or purse, so you can have it handy when you go grocery shopping.

- Buy staple items in bulk. If your family enjoys Chinese meals often, consider buying a large bottle or pack of soy sauce that will last months rather than replacing smaller bottles every other week.

- Buy long-lasting varieties of perishable items. For instance, buy long-life milk and canned vegetables rather than their perishable versions. That way, you always have them handy when you need them without wasting time buying food that will go off before you are ready to eat it. You can also purchase and store them as backups, continuing to use fresh items for your everyday grocery needs.

- Make sure you know in advance what the kids need for their school cookery classes, as a request for ingredients the morning they are required is never helpful.

- Make a habit of sitting down with the family every week to see if there are any extras needed that week - cookery class ingredients, replacement toothpaste, or deodorant are all essential items that don't form part of a weekly shop.

- Use grocery shopping list apps, such as Our Groceries and Bring!, that allow everyone in the family to add items as they run out or to add things they need for the week.

- Shop online to save time and really consider what you want to buy. You can print the basket out and compare it to the goods in your pantry before you check out, thus making sure you haven't forgotten anything or included unnecessary items.

Work Plan

A work plan is similar to the Eisenhower matrix, and it allows you to break down every task you need to complete for work, making it easier for you to accomplish everything. To complete a work plan, jot down your vision for each task. In some cases, the same concept could apply to many different tasks. Your idea could be as simple as "I want to complete this task on time" or "I want to perform well on this task so I can secure a big-name client for my business." Through each step of your work plan, you can look back on your vision to steer you back in the right direction. This will make you more likely to succeed in delivering effective results because your vision will guide every step and decision you take to accomplish this task.

The next step is to write down all your essential work tasks, including milestones, meetings, objectives, questions you need to ask collaborators, clients, managers, delegates, and the timeline and deadline for each milestone. Use the SMART method to make your work plan as specific as possible and to determine all the tasks you need to complete. To make it more transparent, make a note of how you will achieve all these tasks, how long you anticipate it will take you with setbacks, and any obstacles that may prevent you from accomplishing your assignment within the timeline set. Once you have done all this, add all the tasks into the Eisenhower matrix with your visions in mind which will give you a good, solid base on where to place each task on the matrix.

Other practical ways of planning your work schedule are:

- Keep a tidy workspace. It helps to declutter your mind and keep you calm - essential for accomplishing tasks promptly. A clean workspace also reduces distractions.

- Identify times when you go through ego depletion. Organize a break during these times so that you can spend your time effectively.

- Use technology to automate as many tasks as possible. For example, you can use automatically customized emails to respond to frequently sent emails.

A work plan tells you exactly what to do, when to do it, how long you have, and why you are doing it. It cuts to the chase so that your entire focus when working is on your goals.

Children's Schedules

Our children's activities and needs take up a significant part of our time. Time management can help us stay on top of our children's schoolwork and activities and avoid last-minute stress and panic.

You already created a list of all the tasks your children are responsible for when you completed the family's Eisenhower matrix. Discuss these tasks in detail with your children, guiding them with the principles of SMART goals so that they internalize thinking about tasks and responsibilities effectively. If your children are younger, use pictures and drawings to help solidify in their minds the importance of managing their time well. Ask your children to write down or type a list of all the tasks they are responsible for. For example: *"Take the recycling out every night after dinner."* As you write down tasks, list the consequences of competing each task. For example: *"Chris takes the recycling out every night after dinner. We will be very appreciative of Chris for remembering his responsibilities."* Or: *"Ellie needs to complete her homework every night so she gets good grades at school."*

Ask them to write down how long they think each responsibility on their list will take. Then, ask them to record how much time it actually takes. They can then use this information to update the time on their schedule. Use this time strategy to plan your child's regular schedules, such as the morning "getting ready" or "preparing for basketball" routine. This timed routine, once completed, would read something like this:

7:00 am - 7:15 am *Wake up and let the dog out into the backyard.*

7:15 am - 7:30 am *Brush my teeth and use my mouthwash.*

7:30 am - 7:50 am *Take a shower and comb my hair well.*

7:50 am - 8:10 *Get dressed neatly for school.*

8:10 am - 8:30 *Eat breakfast*

8:30 am - 8:40 am *Check that I have all my school supplies in my bag.*

8:40 am - 9:00 am *Walk to school.*

Having a set time allocated to each task gives your child a good structure for how long they should take, challenging them to avoid distractions and keep to their responsibilities. You can change your children's schedules, and the time you set for each task if necessary. The best way to assess if changes are needed is to regularly check in with your children, to discuss what's working and what's not, and to get to the root of any other issues they may be having with their schedules. Regular check-ins are a great way to teach your children the importance of reassessing their time management consistently.

In cases when your children have long-term assignments or projects, spend time with them creating a child-friendly work plan, just like your work plan. Ask them to think about their vision for this assignment. Then, together, make a schedule with all the tasks they need to complete and how much time they need to put the project together. For example, they could take one week to buy supplies., another to research the animal they want to make a sculpture of, and a third to complete the project. You can download worksheets to create assignment work plans with your children. Additionally, you can use chore-sharing apps with your children to streamline the process.

Allow your child to decorate their task list however they want. Once complete, create copies of the list and place them in strategic locations around the house where your child regularly spends time, as a daily reminder to your child to stick to the schedule.

If you have more than one child, turn responsibilities into a friendly competition. Whoever completes most of their tasks without reminders each week gets to pick the pizza toppings for game night or stay up an extra hour at the weekend. Voice your appreciation when your child completes their tasks without prompting as this will keep them motivated. Physical affection when they meet their responsibilities is also a great way to positively reinforce that productive members of the family complete their chores on schedule. Finally, consistently enforce consequences if your child does not meet their responsibilities.

Family Events

Planning family events can be stressful and requires both event planning and time management skills. The first step is to decide on a budget, timeline, and location for the event. Then decide who to invite, what refreshments and entertainment will be needed, and transportation and childcare requirements for the event. Advance planning allows you to identify and address potential issues before they arise, which can help to avoid last-minute mishaps that could impact the success of the event.

The most time-efficient way to plan family events is to use shared family planning and organizer apps which give each family member a way to include their ideas and schedules without having to meet with each other regularly. Consider putting in place a family group chat for discussing issues when planning family events.

Household Chores

As well as sharing tasks amongst the family there are other strategies for planning household chores. Try making a list of your responsibilities and putting it up in the house so your children become familiarized with your household chores after a while. When they see you taking your duties seriously, it motivates them to do the same.

To create your household chore list, divide each responsibility into four categories: daily, weekly, monthly, and those tasks that are less frequent than monthly such as cleaning the windows or the oven. If you are able, outsource some of your duties. For example, you could use a dry cleaning service or a monthly grocery delivery service. Share chores with your partner or any other family member you live with according to which jobs you each prefer or according to who has more free time. We tend to breeze through tasks we enjoy, while those we hate take us longer because we are more likely to be distracted or procrastinate. Our household responsibilities have a way of overwhelming us, building up over time without us realizing it until it is too late. A task list gives you power over your chores so that they are always under your control.

Personal Goals

Plan your personal goals, such as fitness or education goals, in advance and aim to achieve them within a reasonable timeframe. Achieving personal goals can lead to a sense of personal fulfillment and satisfaction. Alongside all your responsibilities, schedule time for yourself so you are investing in your own growth and development, your health and well-being. It is easy to put time for yourself very low down the priority list, so planning in advance helps you gain clarity about what you want to achieve in your personal life and helps you stay motivated.

***

Advance planning involves taking the time to plan and organize your tasks, activities, and commitments ahead of time so that you can use your time more efficiently and effectively. Whether you're a busy professional, student, or parent, advance planning can help you stay on top of your responsibilities, avoid last-minute stress and chaos, and make the most of your time.

Chapter 7

Simplify

Simplification refers to making something simpler or easier. It involves reducing complexity, eliminating unnecessary details, and streamlining processes and can be applied to various aspects of life such as work, personal relationships, and daily routines. In the context of time management, simplification helps us to identify and eliminate time-wasting activities, focus on essential tasks, and reduce distractions. Simplification helps to cut through the weeds and leave space, nutrients, and sunlight for the essential parts of our life to thrive.

Minimalism involves upgrading life by reducing the quantity we pack in but keeping, and even increasing, quality. To do this, we reduce how much clutter is in our lives to create more space for quality. Quality means different things for different people but usually means spending more time at home with family and friends, having more energy for hobbies, spending less time at work, being healthier, and having time to spend on self-care. It operates on the principle that in our modern society, we are too focused on consumerism and too dependent on things to fill the void that relationships with others would usually fill. We replace happiness with consumerism.

Decluttering our home and focusing on buying less can have many benefits including increased productivity, reduced stress, improved decision-making, and increased motivation. Minimalism prioritizes quality over quantity. It is an ideology that believes having one good quality T-shirt is better than having five poor quality T-shirts. The poor quality T-shirts will quickly wear out, meaning you need more time to research and buy new ones. Conversely, the superior quality T-shirt will last a long time, saving you the time it takes to constantly search for and order new ones.

Research is unequivocal: it is experience with people we love and who love us that makes us happy, not the quantity of items we have in our homes. (Schulz & Waldinger, 2023). (Landau, 2023). Not only does simplifying free up our time to pursue the things that matter in life, but it also allows us to destress and rid ourselves of negative emotions and moods that steal our time. When we are stressed, anxious, or sad we cannot focus on our tasks. Simplifying our lives can be a good investment of our time and can give us the space to build relationships and the energy to put into other responsibilities.

How to Simplify Life

Simplification is such a broad concept that it can apply to most areas of our lives. For some people, simplification means that they have a precise meal plan that they follow weekly. By keeping the same meal plan, they don't have to spend time and energy each week deciding on new recipes, browsing the aisles, and trying to find specific ingredients. Following such a system, a family can purchase ingredients in bulk, cutting their food shopping frequency by hours a month.

It could mean reducing our wardrobe to eliminate the decision-making process when choosing what to wear each day or decluttering our physical space by giving away some furniture to cut back on cleaning and upkeep.

Simplification is a lifestyle and a philosophy, so it is up to you to think of ways to adopt that philosophy as perfectly as you can to meet your family's specific needs. Try to think how you could make some of your responsibilities or tasks easier whether cooking, spending time with family, exercising, or working. For example, if you take a significant trip every year with your family, you may decide to vacation closer to home to spend less time planning the trip, going to and from airports, and all the little but essential tasks that travel planning requires. Instead, you can take a vacation only a few miles from home that requires little travel preparation. That way, all the planning and travel time you save can be added to your vacation days, giving you more quality time to relax and enjoy with your family.

Alternatively, you may take stock of your relationships and decide that a couple of your friendships take up too much of your time and energy, forcing you to take time out to recuperate. By simplifying your relationships, you can give less time to these friends, allowing more space for quality family time. Similarly, there may be complications in your life that you decide you no longer need, such as a second property, a sideline business, additional financial accounts you could consolidate, and so on.

These are just some examples of how you can use a minimalist philosophy to benefit yourself and your family. The more you practice, the more it will come naturally to you. Once you get used to it, you will be able to easily find creative ways in which you can apply it to your family's individual needs.

The advantages of adopting a minimalist lifestyle are:

- Saving finite resources. Simplifying your life saves time, money, energy, and even space in your home.

- Decluttering the space around you frees your mind of mental clutter. For example, a decluttered office offers no distraction, so you can concentrate on the task at hand and complete your assignments on time or with time to spare.

- A minimalist mindset teaches you to prioritize what is most important in your life and gives you the ability to free up space in your life for more beneficial things and relationships.

- Simplification is a fabulous way to stay organized. With fewer possessions around, it's easier to keep everything in its place and more difficult for you to lose something.

Introducing Simplification to Your Family

Introducing simplification to your family can be a challenging transitional process. Start by applying it to areas of your personal life to get a feel for how it works and how to use it effectively. Once you begin to see the effects in your personal life, the next step is to champion the benefits to family members. Gently introduce minimalism to your family as a topic of conversation. What do they think of it? Can they think of ways to apply it to their lives? When you give your family members the authority to decide how to use simplification instead of forcing it upon them, they will be more open to change. Minimalism can be a valuable and practical lifestyle for children as well as adults. Here are some ways we can help children to adopt minimalism:

- Teach children the value of experiences over possessions. Encourage them to focus on creating memories and experiences, rather than acquiring more material possessions. This could mean spending quality time together as a family, taking trips, exploring nature, or pursuing hobbies and interests.

- Teach children the importance of decluttering and giving away items they no longer use or need. Help them go through their toys, clothes, and other belongings to decide what to keep, donate, or recycle.

- Limit screen time: Minimalism is not just about physical possessions, but also about reducing digital clutter. Encourage children to limit their screen time and focus on activities that engage them in the real world.

- Prioritize quality over quantity: Encourage children to focus on acquiring high-quality items that will last longer and serve them better, rather than buying cheap, disposable items that will quickly wear out and need to be replaced.

- Set boundaries with gifts: Encourage friends and family to give gifts that align with your family's values and minimalist lifestyle. Encourage them to give experiences, consumables, or gifts that will be useful and long-lasting, rather than cheap trinkets that will quickly be broken or forgotten.

- Encourage children to be mindful of their consumption habits and the impact their choices have on the environment and other people. Help them to make conscious choices that reflect their values, such as buying secondhand, supporting local businesses, or choosing eco-friendly products.

Time management is a lifestyle and a lifelong goal. There is no need to pressure yourself - or your family - into adopting a minimalist approach in the short term.

Materialism is a popular lifestyle choice because it offers us the all-too-addictive dopamine hits that our brains crave. It's why we get excited and happy when we purchase a new item, only to toss it aside like we do the rest of our "junk." However, we can still train our brain and teach it new coping skills. Rather than filling boredom and inner emptiness with material things and purchasing items we don't need, it is possible to train our brain to get its dopamine hits from other sources. The perfect replacement for the happiness and excitement that materialism provides us, is to spend time with the people we love.

If you are worried that a minimalist household will be boring for your children, your fears are unfounded. According to research, children with fewer toys are happier and more creative (Lascala, 2018). Too many toys strip kids of their natural creativity, causing them to play for less time, on average, than kids with fewer toys. The minimalist lifestyle trains your children's brains to be more creative: a skill set that is beneficial for them as they grow older and move on in their education and career. Remember that we have all grown up under a capitalist system that promotes materialism, even when we don't have the money to buy things or the time to take care of them. Consequently, most people are still unable to think and see life outside of the status quo.

Here are some tips that will make simplification work for you and your family:

- Don't give into a scarcity mindset. Many people live a material-istic lifestyle because they fear they won't be able to replace their possessions when needed. Hence the hoarding of toilet rolls that took place during the pandemic. In today's economy of 24-hour delivery, online stores, and an interconnected world where you can purchase items from international sellers, a scarcity mindset should no longer apply.

- Enjoy the simple pleasures of life. Simplification does not auto-matically translate to life without pleasure or joy. A minimalist can still enjoy playing ball with their child, an ice cream cone at the park, or just sitting in the sun on a hot day.

- Be realistic about what you can achieve. If you have several young children, start small by reducing commitments or by decluttering where you can.

- Create routines for daily chores. Routines will help you organize your family's life much more efficiently and effectively.

- Be content. Learn how to wean yourself from the mindset of constantly wanting more.

- Don't beat yourself up. There will be days when you don't meet your expectations and when you give into your brain's demand for dopamine by buying things you do not need. There is no need to beat yourself up for being human. Pick yourself up and keep going. Teach your children that it's ok to make mistakes as long as we learn from them.

- Only have a few rules. If you have too many rules about what you can or can't do, then you have deviated from the principle vision of simplification in the first place.

- Practice mindful gratitude for what you do have. Take time to be fully present and engage in the moment. Mindfulness can help you find joy in simplicity.

- Learn to say no to commitments that do not align with your priorities or bring you joy. Focus on what's most important to you and let go of the things that aren't essential.

***

Simplifying your life and your schedule can be a powerful tool for effective time management. Simplification involves focusing on the things that matter most and eliminating unnecessary clutter, commitments, and distractions from your life. By simplifying your schedule and your commitments, you can create more time and space in your life, reduce stress and overwhelm, and focus on the things that truly matter.

Chapter 8

Multitasking

I n today's fast-paced environment, multitasking has become a buzz-word and is frequently viewed as a desirable quality. In reality, multitasking might actually hinder our capacity to do tasks quickly and effectively as we don't give our all to any of the tasks we take on. Multitasking can be a great skill that most parents do daily without even realizing it. For example, we may have fed the baby a few times while chatting with a friend or been on the phone while cooking dinner for the family. But there is a time and a place for multi-tasking and the skill is to determine when to use this to manage our time, and when to focus our attention on one single task to get that done more effectively.

We can best use multitasking as a time management strategy by identifying pockets of time where we can build in layers of productivity. For example, if that hour-long podcast feels overwhelming because it's so long, you could break it into 10-minute installments and listen while getting dressed in the morning. You may feel that this is a better use of time than taking an hour out of a busy day to sit and entirely focus on the podcast.

Multitasking aims to increase productivity and make the household run more efficiently with our finite time. Multitasking, like outsourcing, is designed to remove as many tasks as possible from our responsibilities list in as little time. Why complete one duty in thirty minutes when we can achieve two simultaneously? Based on how our brains work, we can define multitasking more accurately as alternate, repeated time blocking because we are alternating between two or more tasks quickly, intending to complete them simultaneously.

In the example of feeding the baby while chatting with a friend, although both acts happen simultaneously, we switch our attention periodically from the baby to the conversation. While checking on the baby, we are not mentally present and may miss some of the conversation. This is because multitasking can result in a state of mental overload. Nevertheless, we may fill in the gaps from the information from the rest of our conversation or decide we get the gist of the conversation even with some information missing. You will notice that your brain does this when speaking to someone but also focusing on another task. What you're doing is not multitasking but task switching.

Neuropsychologist Cynthia Kubu describes it as: "When we think we're multitasking, most often we aren't really doing two things at once. But instead, we're doing individual actions in rapid succession, or task-switching" (Ho, 2023).

Multitasking has pros and cons, which determine how best to use it for time management. There are better options for critical and urgent duties that require complete concentration. If you have a job interview, it's not a great idea to multitask by responding to emails during the interview. However, multitasking is great for less important items on your Eisenhower matrix. Although you may lose some quality when carrying out these duties, you can still successfully achieve them without running out of time.

It is better to lose about 10% of quality when performing a task that's not important and urgent than not to complete the job.

We have household duties because they enable the smooth running of every other aspect of our lives. Consistently failing to complete household duties will start a snowball effect, seriously affecting all the areas of your life. You must go food shopping to eat. If you have no food to eat at home, you may pay extra for food delivery, leaving you with little money to spend the rest of the week. Conversely, you can stay hungry, affecting your job performance and putting your job and family's financial security at risk. In other words, in some cases the consequences of not completing a task at all, as opposed to the results of finishing it with 90% quality, are poles apart.

Choose to multitask when suitable. If you're cooking while helping your child with their homework, you may accidentally forget to add a herb. Although this may slightly detract from the taste of your meal, the consequences are not as severe as if your child begins failing at school because of a lack of parental attention at home. And it is easy to fix the taste of a meal by adding herbs afterward.

For duties that are present on the not urgent and not important panel of your Eisenhower matrix, multitasking can be encouraged, whether you are carrying out these duties or someone else in your family. Goals such as, "Take out the recycling" and, "Walk the dog" can be accomplished together if you take the recycling with you on your way out to walk the dog.

To make multitasking effective it must improve your productivity within your timeframe and provide satisfaction, without giving you mental burnout. Here are some tips which you may find useful when determining when to multi-task and when to single-task:

Multi-task during routines that require little mental load.

Daily routines such as showering, getting dressed, walking or driving to work, and taking the dog for a walk are ideal times to multi-task. Build in layers of productivity here by catching up on the phone, listening to training courses, learning a language, or meal planning using a voice-activated shopping list.

Multi-task when you have five minutes to spare.

Waiting for the microwave to ping, waiting in line at the store, sitting at the bus stop can be small pockets of time that we can maximize by multi-tasking. Have a list of activities in mind that you can do when you have five minutes to kill such as:

- Delete apps and unsubscribe from unwanted emails

- Stretch, meditate, breathe, or practice mindfulness

- Read a few pages of a book on Kindle

- Write a note of appreciation to put in your gratitude jar

- Send a quick text to a friend or family member to remind them that they're loved

- Keep the brain active by doing a puzzle or crossword

- Practice a new language or rehearse what you need to say to a colleague

If we build in these mini sessions of productivity 2 or 3 times a day, we will make an extra 1 or 2 hours available each week to include a beneficial activity in our schedule that we might not have otherwise found time for.

<u>Multitask by spending time with your children.</u>

For a happy family life, it is imperative to find ways to connect with our children to build strong relationships, promote positive development, and foster emotional well-being. We can spend time engaging, chatting, and strengthening our bond with them while completing other activities. Multitasking some activities doesn't mean we can't be fully present with them. The following activities can all be done while connecting with our children:

- Cooking together – even spending five minutes with your child showing them how to whip up some guacamole is five minutes of bonding you might otherwise have missed out on.

- Gardening – if you need to weed a bed, make it a competition with your child to see how many weeds you can each pull up.

- Chores – dusting a room together is a great way to catch up on the latest events at school while getting the lounge clean.

- Errands – take your child along for the ride to both help out and engage through conversation.

- Bedtime – while enjoying a cuddle at bedtime, practice mindfulness or encourage them to breathe in sync with you for a calming few minutes of connection.

- Sport –involving our children in our physical activities or taking part in theirs, allows a period of bonding while also getting exercise.

Pros and Cons of Multitasking

Multitasking can be a positive or negative force, depending on how we approach it. If we use it effectively, we will reap benefits such as furthering our connection with our children, maximizing our time, and engaging in activities we might not otherwise have considered. However, we need to be mindful of the potential negatives of multitasking.

Pros

- When we maximize the time we have, we manage our workload more efficiently so feel more in control. Completing all our work on time is a great way to achieve a better work-life balance and free up more time for fun, improving our mental and emotional health. When we fully separate fun time from work, we can lead a more prosperous, happier life.

- While too much mental load is negative, leaning into some cognitive load such as puzzles or listening to podcasts when going through the motions of our normal daily routine, helps us develop mental and emotional resilience. It's partly why some people can withstand more pressure and stress than others: they have developed the mental stamina, brain power, and emotional perseverance needed to take on that challenge.

- Multitasking trains us to put off procrastination by having a list of beneficial activities ready and waiting for when we have a spare five minutes.

- Multitasking works best when we spend our free time training our brains, playing mental and puzzle games, practicing mindfulness, and participating in physical activity.

Cons

- People who multitask constantly are often the people who feel most overloaded. Take breaks from multitasking to avoid mental overload and have periods when you just focus on single-tasking.

- Multitasking can build emotional perseverance, but over-dependence can lead to adverse mental health. If you push yourself past the point where you can withstand the cognitive load, it can cause fears that you are not being successful at tasks, which, can lead to lower productivity in the long term. Make sure you choose the correct moments to multitask and focus on single tasks the rest of the time.

- Multitasking is a focus- and drive-based type of time management, making it particularly effective against procrastination. However, if you are regularly in this state, it promotes a mindset of accomplishing all your tasks as an individual, which is against the spirit of collaboration. There may be days when you need help, so other family members may have to take on your obligations. People who are controlling try to manage how others accomplish the task. People perform tasks differently based on their strengths and weaknesses, so trying to manage others can cause rifts and conflicts within the family, leading to less effective time management in the long term.

The same individually driven dynamic can negatively affect your relationship with your family when you have to work on the same chores together. To combat this, recognize that delegation, outsourcing, and collaboration are all parts of multitasking. Put them into practice regularly to keep up your skills. Learn to accept your limitations, such as your mental capacity, so that you can easily recognize when you need to outsource and delegate for your good - and in the family's interest.

***

In summary, Multitasking is used daily by most parents without even realizing it. To improve productivity and time management, you can multitask more intentionally when you have five minutes to spare or when going about your regular routine. Multitasking can allow more connection with your family by freeing up your time and giving you opportunities to collaborate with them on tasks. It can be an excellent time management hack. However, there are better options for critical and urgent duties that need your complete concentration than multitasking so avoid mental overload by focusing on single tasks where necessary.

Chapter 9

Relax and Have Fun

Our brains are wired to need work, rest, and play. Time management, organization, discipline, and hard work, are important in life, but not the only necessary skillset. We all need to feel emotionally and physically connected with the people we love so emotional skills, social skills, and human connection are just as necessary, to feel content and fulfilled.

Think about how many times you have been offered a job, not because you had the exact skills requirement and qualifications, but because you were able to form a connection with the interviewer. Think about all the relationships you built in your community by attending functions and events which introduced you to new and influential people around you. With the right connections, our lives become not only more accessible but also richer and fuller. Likewise, knowing how to relax and have fun is a great way to be happy and succeed.

Fun is the best way to build the skills to connect with others, even in professional and academic settings. Building connections is a rung on the ladder to your children's success in a world of grade point averages and the race to pick a good college. It helps to spend time with your children, taking them to places, events, and activities where they can socialize with other people to pick up social skills and emotional intelligence.

This chapter investigates how to change our mindset so that we learn to see joy not as an afterthought but as an intentional act. Fun is as essential as everything else on our responsibilities list. Time for fun, activities, family, a partner, relaxation, and self-care should be scheduled and honored. We should ensure we celebrate fun, even with the temptation many of us face to forgo it in search of more quantifiable productivity, such as work performance.

Time with a partner

When couples spend time with each other, they improve their well-being and happiness and reduce their stress. Spending time with your partner benefits you and your partner, your children, and the entire family unit. Despite this, research shows that "Parents share significantly less total and exclusive spousal time than nonparents... Shared time is important for marital well-being and that the quality of marital relationships is associated with the quality of parent-child relationships" (Flood and Genadek, 2017). When you spend time with your partner, you bond and feel connected to them. Correspondingly, when you feel closer to your partner, you become more "in sync" with them.

Being in sync with your partner is a time management superpower. It simplifies your family's organizational processes since you can cover for each other's weaknesses when needed and it cuts back on misunderstandings and arguments. Sharing time allows you to develop a deep appreciation and love for each other. Humans typically try their hardest to understand the people they love and meet them halfway.

For example, if you both completed your Eisenhower matrix for the month, you may come across specific tasks you disagree on. Perhaps your partner thinks you should be responsible for a task because they better fit your schedule, while you think the same task better suits your partner's strengths and character. Rather than coming to a disagreement, you may choose to compromise: you both want what's best for other when you work from a place of deep connection, love, and respect. Using the "in sync" communication you develop from spending time with each other, you can communicate your needs more effectively and promptly. Otherwise, you may both reach an impasse that could result in the family wasting precious time throughout the month. In addition, your children reap the benefit of a much more organized and time-managed household. For example, you can only take your children to their various weekly activities if you and your partner are in sync. Instead, you and your partner may find yourselves late, forgetting events, or needing more time to complete chores.

Despite the benefits of spending time with your partner, it is still a struggle in modern society due to work and, ironically, family constraints. Researchers Flood and Genadek (2017) explain this by writing: "Because work and family are 'greedy' institutions, they are often in conflict. Both work and family have high demands and intensive time commitments... time-based conflict may be especially salient for couples with high work and parenting demands, thereby limiting the time spouses have available to allocate to one another."

Parents expect to successfully balance running the household, being available to their children, meeting work demands and often juggling taking care of their own parents too. However, there are still ways to schedule a time to connect with your partner, such as:

- Powering down.

Date night is a great idea but you don't always have to go out or have a formal date night to spend time with your partner. Setting aside just 20 minutes at the end of the night to talk to each other will do wonders for helping you stay connected. It is also a good idea to power down during this time so turn off electronic devices that could distract you so that your focus is entirely on your partner.

- Spending time without your kids.

You can't power children off like electronic devices, but they can distract you when you want to connect with your partner. It's best to spend isolated time with your partner so that you can communicate with them with honesty that only isolation can guarantee you. Try to spend a few hours with your partner without the kids each month. Take advantage of times when they are not at home, such as when away at camp or at sports practice. You could ask a member of your support network to watch them for a few hours so that you can spend isolated time with your partner. You can also take the same day off every month to spend an entire day together without the kids. Alternatively accompany them to their extracurricular activities together so you can catch up, have a coffee and chat together while your children are occupied.

- Planning ahead.

Be deliberate and make spending time with your partner a priority. Add your intention to connect on your Eisenhower matrix under the urgent tasks and schedule a date and time. If you prioritize your relationship with your partner, everything else will succeed.

Self-Care

Before you can give yourself to your partner, you must have something within you to give. Likewise, to be a present and caring parent to your children, you must have a well from which to draw your love, compassion, empathy, and patience. You need to draw from this well to manage your family's time effectively and keep your household organized.

Enter self-care and "me" time. Like spending time with your partner, "me" time is a responsibility that we should add to the urgent list. Recognize that if your relationship with your partner is the root of your family, then your relationship with yourself is the sunlight and water that nourish the root and causes your family to grow. Without sunlight and water, there can be no plants in the first place.

You can be more flexible when scheduling time for yourself. Like partner time, "me" time does not have to be a grand gesture. Going on a solo vacation abroad might be fun, but it might not be practical or reasonable to do so every month. Instead, a more practical way to plan time for yourself is to find time within your schedule to do things that refill and recharge your emotional, mental, and physical energy.

To make "me" time work for you:

- Spend time in self-reflection every day.

Self-reflection allows you to look inwards to find areas in your life that you may be ignoring to your detriment. For example, you can spend ten minutes every morning after your kids have left for school sitting in quiet solitude and having your morning coffee. Spend this time reflecting or giving time and attention to your thoughts and feelings. Self-reflection is well-suited to multitasking too. You can self-reflect while in the shower, cooking, driving, doing the dishes, and so on.

- Connect with people outside of your family.

Sometimes, the people outside our family can feed areas of ourselves that our family cannot. Spending time with people outside your family also allows your brain a change of environment, which promotes a healthy thought process which, in turn, leads to better time management.

- Power off.

Take time out of your daily schedule to turn all electronic devices off and spend time in that quietness. You could take up a hobby during this time or practice self-reflection. You could meditate, exercise, give yourself a pedicure, or play a sport.

- Take up a new hobby.

A new hobby or challenge promotes intelligence and allows you to get to know yourself better. Hobbies are generally joyful activities that let us find self-fulfillment.

- Spend time healing.

Another great way to become self-aware and emotionally intelligent is to heal from past traumas and painful experiences, which could involve spending time in self-therapy, journalling, opening up to people you love about how you feel, and allowing yourself to cry to release negative emotions.

- Pay attention to fatigue.

Fatigue is your body's way of telling you that you must stop and rest. Pay attention to these warning signals from your body because they could become detrimental. You can't time manage your way out of an extended hospital stay. Developing a chronic disease will severely affect your already limited time. Always remember that prevention is better than cure. Plan a rest day every week where you don't exert yourself with physical exercise and you take some time to focus on self-care instead whether in the form of mindfulness, yoga, or taking a family walk.

- Vocalize your intention and expectations.

Let your family know when you will spend your "me" time and vocalize that you expect them to leave you to yourself unless there is an emergency. Be prepared to enforce this boundary if your family does contact you for non-emergencies during "me" time. Enforcing your limits will allow your family to recognize that "me" time is essential.

- Practice self-care.

Pamper yourself often. Have a spa day, take yourself on a date to a nice restaurant, or splurge on those tickets you've wanted for a while. Do things that bring you happiness so you can be happy and return that happiness to your family.

- It's OK to reschedule.

Sometimes, something more pertinent than "me" time will come up. If that happens, it is acceptable to reschedule as long as you still meet your obligation to yourself at a later date.

***

There will always be a compromise in life. With good time management skills, you can reduce the amount of compromise in your family's life. Recognizing limiting self-beliefs and using the coping strategies above will help you avoid parental burnout. Psychologists say that parental burnout is caused by, "Too much stress and the absence of resources to cope with it. You will burn out only if there is an imbalance between stress and resources" (Abramson, 2021).

Burnout can severely affect your family, causing you to tap out, distance yourself from your family and have no energy to take care of your children (Abramson, 2021). Other ways to prevent burnout include:

- Take little "stolen" moments of self-care away from your family during the day. For example, retreat to your room to practice meditation or yoga.

- Treat yourself with love, respect, and compassion, reject guilt and shame, and tell yourself that it is OK to be human.

- Let go of what you should do and accept what you can do.

- Talk about your negative feelings and stress with people who love you.

Mindfulness Meditation

Mindfulness meditation is a great way to regain your sense of peace and calm during your day. It's a practice that allows you to shed stress and anxiety and return to emotional stability. It works by focusing on deep breathing, a natural way to reduce anxiety and stress, in conjunction with taking yourself out of the moment by paying close attention to things around you or within you.

You can practice mindfulness meditation anywhere. All you need to do is begin by taking deep, full breaths and then be alert to whatever is around or within you that seems to be calling out for your attention. You can pay close attention to your hands and all the lines on your hands and how your fingers join together at your palms. You can decide to pay close attention to a pattern on the floor: the color, texture, shape, and any thoughts and feelings that this pattern evokes within you. You could direct all your focus to the music you're listening to, paying close attention to how the melody affects your emotional and mental state. You could spend a few minutes following the change in your emotional and mental state as the music carries you along.

The goal of mindfulness meditation is to take you out of your present reality into a different reality, giving your brain a mini break from all the stress and responsibilities of life. This mini break does not require you to complete your current tasks; you only need to use your brain to transform you into a different space. However, mindfulness meditation is so effective at giving your brain a mini break that when you return to the present, you have more energy, less stress, and more focus. You can also use mindfulness meditation to go deeper within yourself to discover the roots of your fears, anger, and other negative emotions so that you can guarantee that you are making decisions from a logical and fair base, not from a base riddled with unsolved trauma and pain. By analyzing your emotions, you're also less likely to burn out since negative emotions automatically drain us of our energy.

Family Fun

It's sometimes hard to truly connect with our kids during the day-to-day hustle of our lives. We spend our lives rushing them so they're not late for school; constantly reminding them to brush their teeth, get dressed, and put down their screens; breaking up arguments while the dog howls in the background; and telling them the same things over and over until we collapse, exhausted, in a heap on the sofa at the end of the day. Making time to have fun with our children can be beneficial in many ways. It can help to reduce stress levels, improve communication, increase self-esteem, and provide opportunities for learning and growth. In addition, fun activities provide an excellent opportunity for parents to model positive behavior, such as good sportsmanship, creativity, and problem-solving skills. By engaging in these activities, children are more likely to learn important life skills while also having fun.

Time for family fun focuses your children's attention on you, allowing them to learn life values, such as the importance of being respectful when you speak to people, how to start a conversation with strangers, how to win or lose gracefully, and other such critical social skills that they will need to move through society as they grow older. It also allows you the opportunity to catch up with your kids. If you talk and listen to each other in a relaxed environment, you are more likely to glean better insights into their lives, thoughts, feelings, and experiences. Being emotionally close to your children gives them the understanding that they can rely on you to lead them appropriately. It helps you earn their trust, vital to improving family time management since children naturally follow the lead of adults they respect and trust.

Making time for fun is an opportunity to show appreciation and love for your children without distractions. It allows you to treat them affectionately and encourages them to continue working hard towards their goals. Plan time for family fun around your children's favorite activities and in environments where your children feel comfortable. It is better to have a small amount of good quality family time than plenty of poor-quality family time, where you are not fully present or not having fun with your children.

Do not give up if your children say no. Start small and ask them to help you with a fun activity just for five minutes. Continue to put in the effort to try to spend quality time with your children. It shows how much you care, even if they pretend they do not notice. You can make time for the family by involving them in your everyday routines such as completing chores, cooking, and exercising.

Regular family dinners are a great way to connect and build relationships too. Research shows that "Family dinners are great for the body, the physical health, the brains and academic performance, and the spirit... The mental health benefits are just incredible. Regular family dinners are associated with lower rates of depression, anxiety, substance abuse, eating disorders, tobacco use, early teenage pregnancy, and higher rates of resilience and higher self-esteem" (Anderson, 2020).

Regular mealtimes give children a sense of security, routine, and unity and offer a chance to talk and listen to each other, which can improve communication skills. It allows family members to share their thoughts, feelings, and experiences with each other. It's believed that conversation and engagement during family dinners help to stimulate brain development and improve cognitive abilities. Even if you can't make family dinners daily, a few times a week is fine and even better if the children get involved with preparing and cooking with you.

Spending quality time together helps to strengthen family bonds, which leads to a more harmonious family dynamic. It provides an opportunity for family members to communicate, share experiences, and create memories. Relaxing and having fun with family can be a great stress reliever as it helps to take our mind off work or our anxieties, which in turn can lead to better physical and mental health. Engaging in enjoyable activities with family can improve our overall well-being as laughter and physical activity release endorphins, which can boost mood and reduce anxiety. By prioritizing time with family, we can set a good example for our children and other family members. Scheduling time to relax and have fun with our families demonstrates that we value and prioritize our relationships with them. It can also help us to maintain a strong connection with our loved ones and create memories that we will cherish for years to come.

Chapter 10

Mindset

Let's look at your family as though you were a business organization. We can view time management as equivalent to business management, in other words, how to run your unit effectively and efficiently. If every parent is the CEO of their household they must delegate responsibilities, manage their organization and support others to ensure their organization works efficiently. They manage the business's finances to ensure everyone always has enough money and offer support so that employees may develop and improve. They take care of operations within the business so that it remains organized and runs smoothly.

CEOs are not dictators of their organizations; they are obliged to listen to other members of the company who can put their unique perspectives to use for the improvement of the organization and for achieving its goals. These are all responsibilities that you also carry in your household. And while your children are not your staff members, you are responsible for all their needs, financial and emotional.

As a CEO, your job is not to dictate but to enable those in your care to share their wants, needs, and opinions. Likewise, it is your job to facilitate democracy so that everyone is heard and you can all come to a consensus on how to fix issues in a way that leaves everyone satisfied. CEOs engage with everyone in the organization, giving other people's views importance, listening carefully, implementing suggestions for the organization's operation, and making democratic decisions that make people happy.

Be adaptable

As well as competence, engagement, listening, and democracy, another crucial skill you need for the success of your family unit is adaptability. Research shows that flexible CEOs are 6.7 times more likely to succeed than those who are not (Bothello, 2017). Dominic Barton, a global managing partner of McKinsey & Company, said that adaptability means "Dealing with situations that are not in the playbook. As a CEO, you are constantly faced with situations where a playbook simply cannot exist. You'd better be ready to adapt" (Bothello, 2017).

Being adaptable also means being able to accept setbacks without blaming yourself. Instead, we should view setbacks as pivotal for success. For example, you may have many tasks left the first time you try multitasking and time blocking. Instead of giving up, reassess what caused you to fail at managing your time well. Did you cram too many activities into one day, hoping that you could complete them by multitasking, yet forgetting that you also need to consider mental overload?

Be honest with yourself about where you failed. The Harvard Business Review explains it perfectly: "Adaptable CEOs also recognize that setbacks are an integral part of changing course and treat their mistakes as opportunities to learn and grow. In our sample, CEOs who considered setbacks to be failures had 50% less chance of thriving. Successful CEOs, on the other hand, would offer unabashedly matter-of-fact accounts of where and why they had come up short and give specific examples of how they tweaked their approach to do better next time. Similarly, aspiring CEOs who demonstrated this kind of attitude (what Stanford's Carol Dweck calls a 'growth mindset') were more likely to make it to the top of the pyramid" (Bothello, 2017).

To be adaptable, you must constantly reassess what works and what doesn't, what you need to do better next time, and what you need to keep the same. Just as time management is a mindset and a lifestyle, so is adaptability. It is a skill that requires daily practice to spot your family's strengths and weaknesses, and to turn those weaknesses, ultimately, into strengths for better time management and organization and for achieving your family's goals.

There will be setbacks that you need to approach with a business mindset and setbacks that you need to approach with a loving mindset of a parent or partner. In some instances, you might require an amalgamation of both mindsets. As with anything, your mindset should not be a black-and-white perception of problems. Instead, take in all the gray areas to maximize your family's success.

An adaptable mindset will allow you to continue to work hard towards time management and your family's goals, even in frustrating moments when your methods are unsuccessful, so it should be a continuous effort woven into your lifestyle. In today's fast-paced world, things can change quickly, and you need to be able to adjust your plans and priorities accordingly. By constantly improving your skills and knowledge, you can stay ahead of the curve and be better prepared for any challenges that come your way.

Resilience

Before you can teach your children self-reliance, you must have the qualities needed to make yourself self-reliant. Essential attributes of self-reliance include adaptability, balance, and resilience. Resilience is important because you are guaranteed to face setbacks and failures as you proceed on your time management journey. Resilience will help you persevere and fight for your family when frustrations get to you. We are all familiar with the disappointment of running out of time and the frustrations of a chaotic life. You can develop resilience for these frustrations and failures by using time for self-care, seeking healing and solitude, and incorporating mindfulness meditation into your week.

Another way to develop resilience is to lean into your authenticity as a CEO, partner, and parent—endeavor to get to know yourself better through regular "me" time. The more you know yourself, the more you can find innovative solutions to setbacks that truly work for you. The more you get to know yourself, the more authentic you become and the more specific time management solutions you can develop. By renewing your mindset, you allow your children to emulate and learn from you simply by watching your actions and trying to mimic you. Good CEOs, after all, lead by example.

CEOs may have huge responsibilities, but those who succeed are competent, adaptable, resilient, authentic, and democratic. Unsurprisingly, these qualities make you a great partner and parent, empowering you to create a happy, well-run family. Your children depend on you to lead them, to do what's best for them, and to give them the best life possible. Essentially, they rely on you to produce results and depend on you to be consistent with your commitment.

Growth Mindset

A growth mindset is the belief that you can develop your abilities and intelligence through dedication, hard work, and effort. Developing a growth mindset can enable you to embrace change, let go of perfection and persevere through setbacks. It can help you approach your tasks and goals with a positive and constructive attitude, and you will be more likely to take on challenging projects and not give up.

If your child is constantly evading your attempts to get them to help around the house, don't give in and tell yourself it's not worth the conflict. If you believe that you can make great things happen if you stick at them, if you believe in your goal of their helping to free up more of your time, you will be more inclined to change the methods of enlisting their help and more likely to succeed. That is, you will be more flexible and adaptable to the task at hand.

A person with a growth mindset is more likely to take feedback well and learn from their mistakes, which is how we all want our children to behave. With an attitude of self-belief, you will be less likely to compare yourself to others or measure your success solely based on your achievements, recognizing that growth and progress are just as significant as achieving specific goals.

It is easy to fall into a cycle of enabling our children's weaknesses instead of empowering them to overcome weaknesses and turn them into strengths. It's also often easier to do things yourself rather than to muster up the patience needed to watch your children fail a few times (and sometimes, many times) before they finally master a task. I don't know how many hours I spent reading with my eldest, correcting the same words repeatedly with patience and determination. But now, when I see him relaxed at the end of the day, enjoying a good book, I feel such a sense of achievement, and I know that his love of reading would likely never have developed if I had given up in those early days.

When we allow our children to fail, we allow for their personal growth and development. It may seem counterintuitive, but failure is an essential part of the learning process, and it can teach children critical life skills such as problem-solving, resilience, and perseverance. It can also allow increased enjoyment of activities when there is no pressure to succeed.

Empowering our children may require short-term discipline on our part, but it leads to long-term gain for the whole family. Plus, when we empower our children to take control of their world, we allow them to make mistakes and learn from them, to gain responsibility and confidence in their abilities, and, just as importantly, we free up time that we would typically spend rescuing them from situations such as "I can't find my shirt," or, "Where's my lunchbox?" Sometimes we feel overwhelmed because we struggle to carry out our children's responsibilities on top of our obligations.

When children are allowed to fail, they learn that it is ok to make mistakes and that failure is not the end of the road. Instead, failure can be an opportunity to learn and grow. They determine how to analyze a situation, identify the problem, and think of potential solutions, which helps them develop a growth mindset.

Have a little Patience.

For most parents, getting their children out of the door for school is one of the key times for high-stress levels. Your children are half-dressed, lounging around watching TV while you're frantically throwing books, water bottles, sports equipment, and lunchboxes at them, getting frustrated that they seem incapable of helping. Instead, empower your children by training them to fulfill their responsibilities without your input. When you take the time to teach your children this way, you give them the starting tools they need to become competent leaders.

Use the following solutions to teach your children self-reliance, responsibility, and independence.

- Help your children list the tasks they need to do regularly. They might write down something like the following: get dressed, brush teeth, use mouthwash, fill water bottles, have sports clothes ready for after school, do homework, take the dog out, walk to school, etc. Patiently help your child complete all the tasks for a few weeks or months until it becomes second nature to them. Once it becomes routine, they are less likely to forget to complete a task. By involving yourself in these tasks, you also bring comfort and familiarity to their chores.

- Have a long-term view. Most of the truly important things in life take time to do, such as starting a business, finding true love, bringing up your children, and getting into shape. By developing a long-term view you are more likely to understand that you need to repeat things for many days, weeks, months, and even years to make them stick. But, it is worth the effort if you keep your long-term goal in mind.

- When completing tasks requiring preparation, involve your child at every stage so they understand the importance of always being prepared. For example, involve them in preparing meals for the week so they know how much effort goes into preparation and why it's not appropriate to rely solely on you to prepare them. Allow them to experience the benefits of being well-prepared; for example, if you have enough time not to rush the walk to school, you could play a game along the way. Doing so creates an association in their minds between being prepared and positive outcomes.

- Get done what you can the night before, e.g., put books in your bag, wipe down football shoes, etc. Go through this routine daily with your children, just as you do their regular daily tasks.

- Participating in desirable activities is another excellent way to associate rest time with positivity, enabling your child to understand that, although they may have to fulfill their responsibilities, they can also have daily fun with you. Even five minutes of fun activity time with a parent could be a just reward for your child getting into good habits.

- Practice, practice, practice, and practice some more. Eventually, this routine will become second nature, and you will free up plenty of time for yourself. Even better, you will gain a newfound sense of peace and calm from losing a significant source of your mental overload!

- Resist the temptation to step in and help. Allow your child to fail and live with the consequences of their actions. Your children will only become responsible if they experience the adverse effects of their irresponsibility. It is better to learn the consequences of forgetting their sports kit than it is for them to be rescued by you taking it to school. A better approach is to support them through the consequences of their actions. For instance, if they feel angry that they missed a key match at school because they forgot their sports kit, you can talk them through their anger, support them in releasing their frustration and encourage them to think of methods to help them remember their sports kit next time, like leaving it by the front door or setting a daily reminder on their phone.

- Differentiate between severe consequences and manageable consequences. Your child missing a match for one day is not a severe consequence. Conversely, your child forgetting to set the alarm and missing an exam may have far-reaching consequences. Remember that your children have still-developing brains, so you will need to step up and be responsible if they fail on tasks with severe consequences. Later, you can think of a solution to help your child remember these obligations.

The key to making these teachings stick in your children's minds is repetition. Children, and indeed adults, learn through repetition. Your children also need to recognize that you are teaching them responsibility, not because you're angry at them but because you care about them. They must accept that you are trying to improve their ability as individuals out of your love for them.

Our lessons stick when we teach and raise children from a place of love. If you find yourself saying the same things repeatedly, try to step back so that you don't succumb to frustration. You need resilience and adaptability when teaching your children. Solutions that work successfully on one child may not work with another child because they are different individuals with different needs, personalities, strengths, and weaknesses. Try to be creative and find unique and effective methods of teaching your children self-reliance.

***

Imagine you time block an entire day, ensuring you're not carrying too much of a mental load, following your Eisenhower matrix, keeping time for self-care, and holding back from reminding your children of their responsibilities. You've done everything to implement the correct strategies for time management and organization. And yet, you still have tasks left at the end of the day that you could not complete, some of which are important. You are not a bad parent just because you could not find time to do the laundry this week or because you ordered takeout occasionally when you were too tired to cook. We internalize how we must do it all, but what happens when we can't? We change our mindsets and learn how to pick our battles.

When setbacks in our carefully prepared, time-managed plans happen, it is easy to blame ourselves. After all, we did everything we were supposed to. As parents, we are especially prone to blaming ourselves when we can't do everything right for our families. Maybe you missed your child's recital, even though it was on your essential and urgent list of activities for the day. Perhaps you could not visit an unwell relative this week and feel guilty about that.

Shifting your mindset from lack and failure to progress and success is better. Even though you sometimes don't meet all your responsibilities - even while using time-saving management strategies - it does not mean you are a failure; it simply means that you are human and you are trying your best. Even if you have not made as much progress in the short term, you are still progressing long-term by following a time-management lifestyle. In short, a growth mindset does not ascribe to the belief that human limitation is a failure. By acknowledging that you will always naturally reach limitations and setbacks because you are human, you can plan for this.

Think of it as running a marathon. If you start to get cramps, you may need to pause temporarily to stretch your muscles so that you can finish the race. If you ignore the cramps because you are scared of failing, they will worsen, and you will not be able to complete the marathon. With time management, you are not running a sprint but a lifelong marathon. In essence, there will be times when you need to pause to catch your breath, stretch, hydrate, and rest. With renewed energy and vitality, you can then continue. There are no winners or losers in this race, only those who run the race well.

Let Go of Perfection

It is easy to look at other parents around you who seem to be handling it well, without stress, anxiety, or setbacks. If you compare your life to other families, remember that you are comparing your reality to assumptions. Just because other parents don't seem to struggle with managing their time does not mean they have it all under control. Refrain from comparing your reality to other people's highlight reel. It is natural to make comparisons sometimes - especially if other parents surround you. If you fall into comparison, call yourself back by reminding yourself that comparison is the thief of joy. If it helps you, repeat this mantra: "There are no winners or losers in this race; there are only those who run the race well."

When we let go of the need for perfection, we open ourselves up to more possibilities and opportunities. We allow ourselves to take risks, learn from our mistakes, and ultimately become more efficient in managing our time. By accepting that we cannot be perfect and that mistakes are inevitable, we can reduce stress and increase productivity. Instead of wasting time on perfecting every detail, we can focus on completing tasks to the best of our ability and move on to the next job.

Recognize Limiting Beliefs

Self-doubt is an unfortunate part of the human experience. You want to be your best self, but emotional resilience and self-confidence are finite human resources. Occasionally, you might implement a new solution and wonder if you did the right thing. Sometimes, solutions you try out fail, and you must return to the drawing board. When your confidence is low, limiting beliefs and self-doubt creep in. You may feel like giving up. After all, you're trying so hard and seem only to be meeting with setbacks. You may think that other families are doing much better, prompting you to believe it is because you are terrible at managing your family's time.

Acknowledging your feelings is the most crucial antidote for limiting beliefs and self-doubt. Acknowledge that you are going through a normal human reaction to setbacks and life's general hustle and bustle. Return to your mantra: "There are no winners or losers in this race, only those who run the race well, and I am trying my best." If you need to, take a break to recalibrate and give yourself some space from all your responsibilities. Then, remind yourself why you are doing this: to be a good parent and partner and give your family the best life you can. Acknowledge that this is just a setback. A time-smart mindset acknowledges that there is no such thing as failures but opportunities to learn, improve, grow, and ultimately reach success.

Another coping strategy is to talk things out with your support network. These people know you and your family best, and they can offer advice and perspectives you might not see. Sometimes, it takes a less invested person to breeze in and explore the problem from an external perspective. Even if your support network cannot offer solutions, they can give you the encouragement you need to pull through your setback and provide you with the chance to lighten your mental load, allowing you to think of better ways to manage the situation.

It often helps to think about some of life's most outstanding leaders, some of whom faced incredible setbacks while trying to achieve their goals. Like all of us, they faced self-doubt, and they experienced moments where they blamed themselves for making mistakes or for making decisions that ultimately did not work out. Nonetheless, we remember these people not for these setbacks but because they ran their race well. We recognize the achievements they made because they persevered. They continued to try, building upon the lessons they learned from the setbacks they encountered. As your family's CEO, this adaptability and resilience will allow you to pick yourself up when you get tired.

Chapter 11

Take action

Procrastination is a common behavior that many of us experience at some point in our lives. It's the act of delaying or avoiding a task that needs to be done, often until the last possible moment. Let's say you have a big project due in two weeks. You know you should start working on it right away, but you keep putting it off. Instead, you spend time checking social media, watching TV, or doing other less important things. As the deadline approaches, you start to feel more and more stressed about the project, but you still can't seem to motivate yourself to get started. Finally, a day or two before the deadline, you cram all of your work into a marathon session, staying up late and working frantically to get it all done in time. While you may have finished the project, you probably didn't produce your best work, and you likely experienced a lot of unnecessary stress along the way. Delaying important tasks and instead engaging in less important activities is a classic example of procrastination, causing us to work under pressure and produce subpar results.

It's important to note that procrastination is normal behavior, and it's not always a bad thing. Sometimes, taking a break or delaying a task can be helpful for our mental health and well-being. However, when procrastination becomes a habit that interferes with our productivity and success, we should address it and develop strategies for overcoming it. There are several reasons why we procrastinate, and understanding these reasons can help us manage and overcome the behavior:

- Fear of failure: One of the primary reasons people procrastinate is the fear of failure. When faced with a task that we perceive as complex or challenging, we may feel overwhelmed and anxious about the outcome. This fear of failure can be so intense that we delay starting the task altogether or engage in other activities to distract ourselves from the task at hand.

- Lack of motivation: Sometimes, we may need more inspiration to get started. In this case, procrastination may be due to a lack of interest in the task, a lack of understanding of how to complete it, or a lack of enthusiasm about the outcome.

- Perfectionism: Perfectionism is the belief that everything we do must be perfect and that anything less is a failure. When we hold ourselves to these impossibly high standards, we may procrastinate because we're afraid of making mistakes or producing work that's less than perfect.

- Overwhelmed by tasks: When faced with multiple jobs, we may become overwhelmed and need guidance on where to start. This feeling of overwhelm can lead to procrastination, as we delay beginning any tasks to avoid stress and pressure.

Taking action is the ultimate goal. We can spend days planning and writing lists of tasks and responsibilities, but unless we take action, we achieve little. Procrastination can take many different forms. You might delay getting started because the job seems overwhelming, or you are scared of failure.

You might be unsure how to proceed with a task or might not be motivated enough to start. Procrastination can also take the form of "being busy" instead of actually completing the task at hand, which can make us feel like we're being productive, but in reality, we're avoiding the job that needs doing. To overcome our tendency to procrastinate, we can follow some of the advice in previous chapters, such as planning, setting realistic deadlines, minimizing distractions, and sharing the workload. When we hold ourselves accountable by tracking and celebrating our progress, we are more likely to stick to the course and continue taking action.

But the best advice is to "Just do it." If you tend to say things like, "Oh, I must fix that," and find yourself saying the same thing again and again but never actually mending it, you are procrastinating. Whenever you walk past the sink thinking, "That really needs a clean," and catch yourself thinking the same thing several times a day, you are suffering from procrastination. What is stopping you from taking action and getting a cloth out to clean the sink? Whenever you find yourself thinking of an action you need to do, either do it or remind yourself to do it at a more convenient time later that day. That way, the situation doesn't get worse, and you don't feel frustrated that you keep forgetting or never find time to do the task.

When we deliberately take action, we can make progress toward our goals. Without action, our goals remain dreams or wishes that never become a reality. By taking action, we're able to turn our aspirations into tangible achievements; we create and build momentum. Each small step we take toward our goals gives us a sense of progress and achievement, which motivates us to keep going. Momentum helps us stay focused, motivated, and energized. Taking action allows us to seize opportunities as they arise. Opportunities don't always present themselves at the most convenient times, and if we're not ready to take action, we may miss out on them. By taking action, we're able to seize opportunities and create our own luck.

Here are some reasons why taking action rather than procrastinating should be our goal:

- Increased productivity: When we take action instead of procrastinating, we can get more done in less time, resulting in increased productivity and a greater sense of accomplishment.

- Reduced stress: Procrastination can cause stress and anxiety, which can negatively impact our mental and physical health. Taking action can help reduce this stress and anxiety by giving us a sense of control over our tasks.

- Improved time management: When we take action instead of procrastinating, we can better manage our time, which can help us avoid feeling overwhelmed by our tasks and give us more time to do the things we enjoy.

- Improved relationships: Procrastination can cause us to miss deadlines or let people down, which can negatively impact our relationships. Taking action and following through on commitments can help us build stronger relationships and trust.

- Greater success: Taking action can lead to greater success in all areas of life. Whether it's achieving our goals at work or in our personal lives, it is is essential for making progress and achieving success.

- Increased self-confidence: When we take action and complete tasks, we feel a sense of accomplishment and pride in our abilities. This can help boost our self-confidence and motivate us to tackle even more significant challenges in the future.

Taking action is one of the most important things you can do to achieve your goals and create the life you want. When you take action, you move forward and make progress. Remember, taking action is a habit, and like any habit, it takes time to develop. Start small and build momentum over time. The more you take action, the easier it will become. And before you know it, you'll be making progress toward your goals and living the life you've always wanted.

Create a Sense of Urgency

Creating a sense of urgency can help us overcome procrastination and take action toward our goals. When we feel a sense of urgency, we're more motivated to act quickly and decisively, which can help us achieve our goals faster and more efficiently. If we are mindful of creating a sense of urgency when completing tasks, we are less likely to dawdle, get distracted, and are more likely to accomplish the goals within the deadline set. You could use a timer to set a specific amount of time for your task. Timers can be a fun and effective way to create a sense of urgency for children. Encourage them to race against the clock to complete a task and offer rewards for finishing before the timer goes off. Likewise, turning chores into a game can make them more enjoyable and create a sense of urgency. Challenge children to see how quickly they can tidy their room or complete their homework and offer rewards for finishing swiftly and accurately.

Another way of creating a sense of urgency is to visualize the consequences of inaction: Sometimes, visualizing the adverse effects of not taking action can create a sense of urgency. Imagine what will happen if you don't take action toward your goals and how that will impact your life in the long run. Visualization can be a powerful motivator to take action and avoid procrastination. Help children understand the benefits of completing tasks quickly and efficiently and what any negative consequences might be. For example, finishing homework early or quickly completing chores can free up time for other things but dawdling, putting things off, or doing a half-hearted job will take longer, leaving less time for fun activities afterward.

Step Out of the Comfort Zone

One of the main reasons we procrastinate is because we are nervous about trying new things, and we are scared of failing. We need to get used to stepping out of our comfort zone and challenging ourselves to do something outside our habits, routines, or experiences. Taking risks and trying new things may be unfamiliar, uncomfortable, or challenging, but personal growth and development come from pushing ourselves beyond what we know. We must take calculated risks, challenge our assumptions and beliefs, and face our fears in order to grow and develop as individuals. Trying a new hobby or sport, speaking in public, traveling to a new country, starting a business, or making a significant life change are actions that may be uncomfortable because they require us to stretch beyond our current level of comfort and familiarity.

Children are constantly stepping out of their comfort zone with everything that life throws at them – starting a new school or club, meeting new people, speaking to adults, learning new skills, and even trying new food. Trying new things and taking risks can help children develop new skills, such as problem-solving, communication, and creativity. When children try new things and succeed, they gain confidence in their abilities and become more willing to take on new challenges in the future. Stepping out of the comfort zone also involves the possibility of failure. Children who experience failure and learn how to cope with it healthily are more resilient and better equipped to handle challenges in the future. Stepping out of the comfort zone can also help children discover their passions and interests, which can lead to lifelong pursuits and hobbies.

When we learn to get comfortable with discomfort and see it as something beneficial that helps us grow and learn, we are less likely to procrastinate and more inclined to relish taking action. Stepping out of our comfort zone can be scary and intimidating, but doing so can help build resilience. When we push ourselves to try new things and face our fears, we become more confident in our abilities and more resilient in the face of challenges. When we try new things, we open ourselves up to new people, places, and experiences, which can be enriching and fulfilling. Face your fears, expect failure, celebrate the journey, and expand your horizons; taking action is the message you need to carry with you to become a more confident, resilient, and productive individual.

Chapter 12

Develop the habit

It is easy to have good intentions. Your good intentions may involve continuously planning your activities by time blocking and mapping out on an Eisenhower matrix. It may mean sitting down with the children and putting a plan in place to share the household chores. It may mean committing to simplifying your life so you can spend more time with your kids, or it may mean putting a list of beneficial activities into place to multitask when you've got five minutes to spare.

But good intentions can often be short-lived, and it is easy to slip back into our regular habits. Soon we are shouting at our children to come and do their chores or giving up and doing them ourselves; we realize at the end of the day that we have spent too long scrolling social media and forgotten about a deadline, or we fail to put our screens down when we intended to connect with our partner. We need to build good habits to permanently put all our newly learned time management skills into place.

In my previous book Mindfulness for Families, we looked at the importance of building habits into routines to make practicing mindfulness a learned, automatic behavior. We can do the same with our time management skills, and it is worth looking at habits and routines again here.

A behavior that is practiced repeatedly becomes habitual and automated as a result. We develop habits in reaction to environmental cues or triggers, and incentives or successful results can reinforce them. To make good time management a habit, create associated triggers initially, repeat the behavior frequently and routinely, and then establish a rewards system for engaging in that habit.

Triggers

Triggers can be visual, technological, or mental. An example of visual cues would be notes left around the house which remind you to do an action at a particular time of day. You could write a specific reminder on a post-it note, such as, "Put ingredients in the slow cooker for tonight's meal," and stick it on the kitchen door so that when you go for your breakfast the following day, you remember your task. Or you could leave less specific instructions, such as, "Take time for self-care every day," or leave notes for the children reminding them of their agreements.

Notifications on your phone are an example of a technological cue. The notification alert prompts you to pick up your phone and check the message. Create diary entries in your shared calendar or set alarms on your phone to remind you to accomplish something. Plan out time on your schedule for fun activities with your kids, time with a partner, and time for yourself.

Mental cues are internal signals that direct our behavior. They assist us in recalling specific information or taking particular actions. Several hundred mental cues are already hardwired in your brain; you can learn new ones through practice or experience. How often do certain sounds, smells, or items bring back particular memories or events? We can learn to manage our reactions to specific situations and utilize that power to our advantage by becoming aware of our mental cues.

By connecting a particular daily behavior to the new habit we hope to establish, we might establish a mental cue. For example, if you intend to do five minutes of stretching every day, you could associate the stretching routine with getting up from your desk. Once the association is established, doing the stretching exercises right away after getting up from your desk will become automatic. For the first month, leave a post-it note on your desk, but after that, you should have formed the habit and be able to continue your practice without a visual reminder.

Commitment and Repetition

To make your new time management habits permanent:

- Commit to a period of at least thirty days.

- Purchase a journal to track your development during this time and keep it wherever you spend your evening so it serves as a daily reminder to write in it.

- Use an app or a reminder on your phone to help you stick with the practice.

- Make sure your family is supportive and will hold you responsible for performing the action again.

"Neuroplasticity," or the brain's capacity to modify and adapt in response to experiences, creates habits and routines that get firmly established in our neural pathways and is essential for learning and memory development. Our brain develops neural connections that link the cue or trigger for a behavior to the action itself when we carry it out, such as brushing our teeth or going for a stroll. By reinforcing these neural connections with each repetition, we make the behavior more automatic. The ability to multitask and be more productive arises from the brain's ability to become so effective at performing the action over time that it takes less conscious effort and attention. According to research, up to 45% of our daily actions are automatic, meaning that we don't give them any conscious thought or intention.

We must act repeatedly and consistently over an extended period for it to become a habit. Once we establish the pattern, the action becomes second nature, and it becomes unnatural not to perform the ritual. For instance, if you set a goal of walking up the escalator on the way to work for a month instead of standing still, and you commit to it, you will eventually discover that you cannot stand still on the escalator; it just feels unnatural. The habit has become ingrained in your life. Try to develop the practice of setting aside a short amount of time each day to plan and prioritize your calendar. Developing a skill that will make us feel more organized and in control will enable us to get rid of the overwhelm and experience more, much like healthy eating, fresh air, exercise, reading, and any other beneficial habit.

Rewards system

The brain's reward system plays a role in the science of routines and habits. Our brain releases dopamine when we act in a way that will result in a reward or pleasant consequence, like feeling good about finishing our to-do list. This neurotransmitter is linked to reward and pleasure, which reinforces the behavior and increases the likelihood that we will repeat it in the future.

- Spend some time picturing yourself attaining your objective. Use the thought of how it will feel to achieve your aim as inspiration to keep going. Write down your thoughts after asking yourself what kind of person you want to be.

- Consider your accomplishments as you move closer to your objective, give yourself a pat on the back, and frequently review your journalling to gauge your progress. Perhaps you'll note in your journal that you'd like to have more control over your life.

- Consider your planning and prioritization each day, and compliment yourself on your efforts. Consider how far you've gone and treat yourself each time you accomplish a goal. A simple gold star in your diary or rewarding yourself with a fun activity or snack could celebrate your progress.

- Celebrate your accomplishments with people who support you as a way to stay inspired and responsible. Reward your kids for supporting your time management objectives. Encouragement, praise, and tangible prizes like a new pen or notebook can help them understand your goal and increase their delight. Spending time with relaxed and content parents is generally the best reward for children, so make sure you give daily one-on-one time priority and build in fun activities to do together.

Daily Routines

Our new habits will eventually be incorporated into our routines, allowing life to operate more smoothly and letting us spend more time together as a family. A routine is a collection of actions we consistently carry out in a specific order or sequence. Routines provide us with a sense of regularity and control over our lives, as well as assisting us in managing our time. Our mental health and well-being can benefit from routines because they can lower stress and anxiety, boost productivity and efficiency, and enhance our general quality of life.

Routines help children and parents feel organized, decrease stress levels, and make time for fun. Routines also help children feel safe, learn life skills, and form healthy habits. Plan predictable and consistent routines so that your children may use them as markers for what is essential to your family. Enjoyable routines centered around family time give kids a sense of belonging and bolster family ties.

Here are some pointers for pulling your time management goals together into new routines:

- Start small: Starting with modest, doable objectives is crucial because developing new habits can be difficult. Set reasonable goals for yourself and pick one or two habits to work on at a time. The five-minute rule states that we can achieve anything if we set aside five minutes each day for it.

- Be consistent: When establishing new routines and habits, consistency is crucial. Commit to carrying out your new routine or habit every day, even if it takes only a few minutes. To ensure that everyone in your family follows the new rule, create a family contract.

- Be persistent: There will inevitably be some opposition to introducing a new habit into your family's routine. Your kids can balk at helping with the duties around the house. Keep trying, and don't give up! The disputes will fade over time, and your family will come to appreciate and benefit from the new routine.

- Use cues: You can remember to practice your new habit or routine by using cues or triggers. Select a signal connected to the desired behavior, such as stretching after leaving your desk.

- Track your progress: You can observe the effects of your new habit or routine over time by keeping track of your progress to stay motivated. Use a monitoring tool or journal to keep track and reflect on any difficulties or victories.

- Embrace self-compassion: Setting up new routines and habits can be difficult, and failures are common. Be supportive and kind to yourself, and remember that every day presents a fresh chance to practice and grow.

- Get support: Surround yourself with people who will encourage and hold you accountable. Find an accountability partner who can support and encourage you as you work towards your goals.

By incorporating these suggestions into your everyday life, you can develop new routines and habits that improve your general well-being, help you manage your life, and lower stress and anxiety.

***

Obstacles

It can be challenging to establish new routines and habits, and numerous barriers may stand in the way. Here are some typical obstacles and advice for getting around them:

- Insufficient motivation: When establishing new routines and habits, it is not easy to stay motivated, especially if you don't experience any immediate benefits. To get beyond this barrier, keep your attention on the long-term advantages of your new routine or practice and keep your goals and motivation in mind.

- Opposition to change: Establishing new routines and habits might be challenging as our minds are programmed to resist change. As you work towards your goals, concentrate on making small, gradual changes and practice patience with yourself. Celebrate minor victories along the road to maintain momentum and drive.

- Lack of support: Explain your vision and goals to your family and get their buy-in. Getting your family's buy-in is important because it creates a sense of ownership and accountability for the time management plan. When everyone is on board and committed to the program, it becomes easier to implement and maintain.

- Perfectionism: Striving for perfection and having high standards can be a significant barrier to forming new habits. Practice self-compassion and put more emphasis on progress than perfection to get beyond this challenge. Keep in mind that failures are to be expected when creating new routines.

By recognizing these obstacles and developing strategies to overcome them, you can create new habits and routines that support your overall well-being and enhance your quality of life.

Chapter 13

Final Words

For all busy parents, time management should be an essential aspect of modern family life. It can be challenging to balance the demands of work, school, and family life, and it requires a specific combination of skills, including effective communication, prioritization, and organization. Effective time management has numerous benefits, including stronger family bonds, improved mental and physical health, and greater overall satisfaction with life. By setting priorities, communicating well, and making the most of the time we have together, we can create a more harmonious, fulfilling life. Whether it's setting aside dedicated family time, delegating tasks, or learning to say "no" to outside obligations, there are many strategies we can use to achieve better time management skills. Above all, managing family time effectively requires a commitment to making spending time together a priority. By recognizing the value of family time and dedicating ourselves to creating more of it, we can reap the rewards of stronger family bonds, more meaningful connections, and a greater sense of overall fulfillment in our lives.

Throughout this book, we have covered some of the key principles of time management. We have seen that assessing our responsibilities and keeping track of our actions enables us to identify time wasters and decide how we should spend our time. We have studied tools to help us prioritize our activities, such as SMART goals and the Eisenhower matrix. We have looked at sharing our load with family or a support network, specifically, how to encourage our kids to contribute to the household. We have examined how embracing technology can help us spend less time on some tasks through automation and outsourcing. We have learned that planning can allow us to save time, feel more organized, and stay in control, especially around household chores such as cooking and shopping. We have studied the principles of simplifying our lives through adopting minimalism, decluttering, and learning to say no, and we have also seen when and when not to multitask.

But these time management principles are only effective if we find balance in our lives. We need to manage our time effectively when necessary but sit back, take a breath, and relax when our bodies tell us to. Assess your time – do you want to multitask by sending emails when you're waiting for the train, or do you want to simply take in the sights and sounds around you and relax your mind? Do you need to volunteer at that event, or have you agreed to help out of guilt? Do what feels right to you, but do it mindfully and with intention.

Time management, as we have seen, is a way to manage life, to make life less chaotic, to avoid burnout, and to enjoy essential things such as time with your partner and children. So make sure your goals are realistic, share your load, spend crucial time planning, let go of perfection and guilt and say yes to fun, enjoyment, relaxation, and fulfilling opportunities. In doing so, you prepare your children for a happy and well-run life in the future. Effective time management connects your family, and a connected family, in turn, improves your time management. Try to develop an adaptable mindset so you learn not to be afraid of failure. Adopting a growth mindset will allow you to create the confidence to step out of your comfort zone and take action. And finally, try to make the tools of time management stick by building them into permanent habits and routines.

Breathe! There is no need to juggle it all and toil away in debtor's prison anymore. Put down the weight you have been carrying and shake your shoulders loose. Shed any guilt because you could not meet all your parental responsibilities in the past and smile because you are about to feel more in control, more confident, more resilient, and happier with your life. You have all the equipment you need to manage not just your time but your life more effectively.

As you embark on your journey towards better family time management, remember to stay flexible, be patient, and, above all, enjoy the time you have together. By managing your time effectively in your daily routine, you can create a happy, close-knit, and healthy family. So go ahead, take the first step towards better family time management today, and teach your children how to become more organized, more connected, and more fulfilled for years to come.

Chapter 14

References

1 6 Effective Prioritization And Time Management Strategies. (2023). HourStack.

Abramson, A. (2021). The impact of parental burnout: What psychological research suggests about how to recognize and overcome it. *American Psychological Association, 52*(7), 36.

Acuity Training. (2022). *Time Management Statistics & Facts (New 2022 Research).* Acuity Training.

Anderson, J. (2020, April 1). *Harvard EdCast: The Benefit of Family Mealtime.* Harvard.

Avada. (2023, March 23). *Multitasking Mom: The Complete Guide to Improve Productivity.* Avada.

AZ Quotes. (2023). *By failing to prepare...* AZ Quotes.

Beckett, K. (2022, May 14). *20 things to buy for meal prepping.* Mealley.

Botelho, E. L. (2017, July 18). *4 Things That Set Successful CEOs Apart.* Harvard Business Review.

Bowman, E. (2012). *Top 8 Time Management Apps for Busy Parents.* ParentMap.

Bungalow. (2023). *The complete Household Chore List.* Bungalow.

Chorney-Booth, E. (2017, May 2). *8 time-saving apps - Today's Parent.* Today's Parent.

Clark, D. (2020, October 24). *Track Your Time for 30 Days. What You Learn Might Surprise You.* Harvard Business Review.

Clockify. (2023). *Time management statistics everyone should know in 2023 (and beyond).* Clockify.

Creating and Applying Schedules to Your Child's Everyday Life. (2021, November 19). INCLUDEnyc.

Cvent. (2023, February 6). *Event Planning Guide with Checklist 2023.* Cvent.

Dickinson, K. (2022, November 23). *Time is money. No time is far more valuable. Here's how to spend money to optimize your time.* Big Think.

Duncan, R. D. (2020, May 22). *You Can't Do It All, And That's Perfectly OK.* Forbes.

E. (2018, May 29). *6 Tips For Building A Strong Support Network From Unlikely Sources.* Forbes.

Estroff, S. D. (2023). *The Age-by-Age Guide to Teaching Kids Time Management.* Scholastic.

Feyoh, M. (2023, February 28). *15 Best Shared Family Calendar Apps & Organizers [2023 Update].* Develop Good Habits.

Flood, S. M., & Genadek, K. R. (2016). Time for Each Other: Work and Family Constraints Among Couples. *Journal of Marriage and Family*, 78(1), 142–164.

Friedman, S. D. (2018, November 14). *How Our Careers Affect Our Children*. Harvard Business Review.

Gilmer, M. (2023, January 9). *Embracing Meditation and Mindfulness in a Busy World*. Cleveland Clinic.

Good Reads. (2023). *Time Management Quotes*. Good Reads.

Gordon, S. (2020, December 8). *How to Use Time Blocking to Manage Your Day*. Verywell Mind.

Greenwald, W. (2023, March 7). *The Best Smart Displays for 2023*. PC-MAG.

Griffeth, L. L. (2023). *Time Management: 10 Strategies for Better Time Management*. UGA Cooperative Extension.

Griffin, M. (2022, December 20). *The 12 tips that will improve your multitasking skills!* Cirkus.

Grose, J. (2020, April 15). How to Avoid Burnout When You Have Little Ones. *The New York Times*.

Ho, L. (2023). *Why Multitasking is Counterproductive and What to Do Instead*. Lifehack.

Hodges, C. (2019, October 7). *A Beginner's Guide to Meal Prep*. Eating Well.

Holt, C., & Holt, C. (2018, July 9). *SheKnows*. SheKnows.

Hrubenja, A. (2022, September 25). *How to Meal Prep - The Ultimate Guide.* Modern Gentlemen.

Indeed Editorial Team. (2022). How To Develop Your Multitasking Skills (With Examples). *Indeed Career Guide.*

Indeed Editorial Team. (2022, June 24). *Time Management Goals To Take Control of Your Time (With Examples).* Indeed Career Guide.

Indeed Editorial Team. (2023). *How To Multitask: 16 Ways To Do It Effectively.* Indeed Career Guide.

Indeed Editorial Team. (2023, February 27). *Hot to Organize Your Day at Work: 15 Tips for Success.* Indeed Career Guide.

Jones, T. (2023, February 18). *The 10 Best Family Organizer Apps of 2023.* FamiSafe.

Klahre, A.M. (2019, July 7). *This is the Magic Number When it Comes to Cleaning.* The Kitchn.

Kristenson, S. (2023, March 15). *11 SMART Goals Examples for Time Management & Productivity.* Develop Good Habits.

Landau, E. (2023). *Study: Experiences make us happier than possessions - CNN.com.* CNN.

Lee, M. (2019, April 16). *A Family App for All: The 11 Best Apps for the Whole Family.* FamilyApp.

Marissa. (2022, June 18). *Family Simplification: 20+ Pros, Cons, and Tips for Simple Living as a Family.* A To Zen Life.

Martin, L., & Martin, L. (2023, March 24). *What is time blocking and how does it work?* Time Doctor Blog.

Miller, A. (2019, December 9). *25 Benefits of Creating a Schedule for Your Tasks. Calendar.*

Miller, D., Waldfogel, J., & Han, W. J. (2012). Family Meals and Child Academic and Behavioral Outcomes. *Child Development*, 83(6), 2104–2120.

Simplification. (2020, October 30). *51 minimalist living tips that lead to a simple life*. Simplification.

Nolan, J. (2018, July 12). *Importance of Quality Time in a Relationship.* The Healthy Marriage.

Nordberg, A. (2020, January 6). *Why kids need a strong network of supportive adults, and how to build that tribe*. Washington Post.

Ozbay, F., Johnson, D. B., Dimoulas, E., Morgan, C., Charney, D. S., & Southwick, S. M. (2007). Social support and resilience to stress: from neurobiology to clinical practice. *Psychiatry* (Edgmont (Pa. : Township)).

P. (2022, April 6). *How To Build A Strong Social Support Network (Complete Guide)*. Inner Toxic Relief.

Panel, E. (2021, September 20). *17 Experts Share Technologies Making A Positive Impact On Society*. Forbes.

Picard, C. (2020, April 10). *10 Best Grocery Shopping List Apps, According to Nutrition and Tech Experts*. Good Housekeeping.

PCMag. (2022c, November 22). *The Best Smart Home Devices for 2023.* PCMAG.

Petre, A. (2018, September 30). *How to Meal Prep - A Beginner's Guide.* Healthline.

Pinsker, J. (2022, December 28). *Don't Just Spend Your Time—Invest It.* WSJ.

Reisenwitz, C. (2022, November 26). *Eisenhower Matrix Guide for Time Management.* Clockwise Inc.

Samphy, Y. (2023, March 8). *16 Effects Of Poor Time Management (Backed By Science).* Y Samphy.

Scholastic Parents Staff. (2023). *9 Ways to Make Household Chores Fun.*

Schulz, M., & Waldinger, R. (2023, February 10). An 85-year Harvard study found the No. 1 thing that makes us happy in life: It helps us "live longer." *CNBC.*

Scroggs, L. (2023). *Avoid the "Urgency Trap" with the Eisenhower Matrix.* Todoist.

Scroggs, L. (2023). *The Complete Guide to Time Blocking.* Todoist.

Simplicity, B. T. (2023). Simplification and Time Management: How The Minimalist Lifestyle Can Improve Your Productivity. *BALANCE THROUGH SIMPLICITY.*

Singh, H. (2017, October 2). *Family Time: Why Spending Time With Family is Important.* Aha Now.

Solan, M. (2021). *Evoking calm: Practicing mindfulness in daily life helps.* Harvard Health.

Soukup, R. (2020). S*top Feeling Guilty When You Can't Do It All (And Do This Instead).* Living Well Spending Less.

Stibich, M., PhD. (2020). *How to Fit Meditation Into Your Day.* Verywell Mind.

Taylor, DP. (2022, August 5). *How to Create the Ultimate Work Plan.* Fool. .

The mindsets and practices of excellent CEOs. (2019, October 25). McKinsey & Company.

Vila, J. (2021). Social Support and Longevity: Meta-Analysis-Based Evidence and Psychobiological Mechanisms. *Frontiers in Psychology, 12.*

Whillans, A. V., & Weidman, A. C. (2016). Valuing Time Over Money Is Associated With Greater Happiness. *Social Psychological and Personality Science, 7*(3), 213–222.

Writer, S. (2023, February 2). *Planning Your Family Engagement Event.* Kaplan Early Learning Company.

About Author

Bethany Fox is an educator and writer originally from the North of England. She has a bachelors in English and a Master of Arts in Film Studies. She lives with her husband and three children on a smallholding in Portland, Oregon. When she is not writing, she spends most of her time cooking, gardening, looking after her flock of chickens and watching her favorite classic movies. And of course, having lots of fun with her kids!

Keep in touch with Bethany via the web: https://www.bethanyfox.com